AF413013

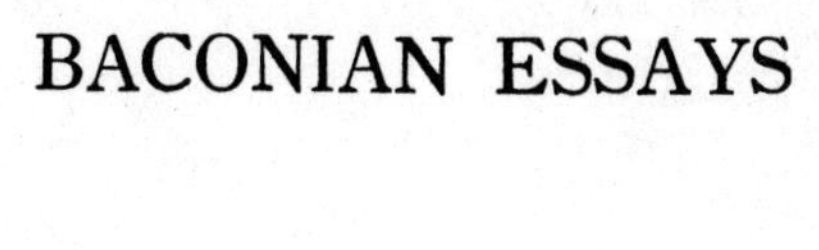

BACONIAN ESSAYS

BACONIAN ESSAYS

BY

E. W. SMITHSON

WITH AN INTRODUCTION AND TWO ESSAYS

BY

SIR GEORGE GREENWOOD

KENNIKAT PRESS
Port Washington, N. Y./London

BACONIAN ESSAYS

First published in 1922
Reissued in 1970 by Kennikat Press
Library of Congress Catalog Card No: 77-105836
ISBN 0-8046-1034-7

Manufactured by Taylor Publishing Company   Dallas, Texas

CONTENTS

BACONIAN ESSAYS

INTRODUCTORY

HENRY JAMES, in a letter to Miss Violet Hunt, thus delivers himself with regard to the authorship of the plays and poems of " Shakespeare " * :—" I am ' a sort of ' haunted by the conviction that the divine William is the biggest and most successful fraud ever practised on a patient world. The more I turn him round and round the more he so affects me."

Now I do not for a moment suppose that in so writing the late Mr. Henry James had any intention of affixing the stigma of personal fraud upon William Shakspere of Stratford-upon-Avon. Doubtless he used the term " fraud " in a semi-jocular vein as we so often hear it made use of in the colloquial language of the present day, and his meaning is nothing more, and nothing less, than this, viz., that the belief that the plays and poems of " Shakespeare " were, in truth and in fact, the work of " the man from Stratford," (as he subsequently, in the same letter, styles " the divine William ") is one of the greatest of all the many delusions which have,

* Letters of Henry James. Macmillan, 1920, Vol. I., p. 432.

from time to time, afflicted a credulous and " a patient world." He believed that when, in the year 1593, the dedication of *Venus and Adonis* to the Young Earl of Southampton was signed " William Shakespeare," that signature did not, in truth and in fact, stand for the Stratford player who never so signed himself, but for a very different person, in quite another sphere of life, who desired to preserve his anonymity. He believed that when plays were published in the name of " Shake-speare " that name did not, in truth and in fact, stand for " the man from Stratford," but again for that same person —or it might be, and in certain cases certainly was, for some other—who desired to publish plays under the mask of a convenient pen-name. And if the authorship of these poems and plays came, in course of time, to be attributed to William Shakspere, the player from Stratford-upon-Avon, who himself never uttered a word, or wrote a syllable, or took any steps whatever to claim the authorship of those poems and plays for himself, but was content merely to play the part of " William the Silent " from first to last, there is, surely, no reason to brand him as a cheat and a " fraud " upon that account, and we may be quite sure that that highly-gifted and distinguished man of literature, Henry James— one of the intellectuals of our day—had no intention of so branding him.

A lady, a short time ago, wrote a book to explain the play of *Hamlet* in quite a new light, by making reference to the special political circumstances of the time when it appeared, such as the " Scottish succession," the character

INTRODUCTORY

of James I, certain events in the lives of Mary Queen of Scots, Burleigh, Essex, Southampton, Elizabeth Vernon, and other historical figures, and producing " detailed analogies between episodes of contemporary history and the play,"* and, in reply to certain objections raised by a well-known critic, she essayed to justify herself by an appeal to the doctrine of " Relativity," which, as she declared with some warmth, had come to stay whether her captious critic wanted it or not !

This lofty invocation of Einstein's theory of Time, Space, and the Universe—a theory so difficult of comprehension that only a favoured few can even affect to understand it—in support of a new interpretation of one of Shakespeare's plays, was, certainly, somewhat ridiculous, but the lady was quite right in her contention—which would equally hold good though Einstein had never lived or taught —that in forming our judgments on men long gone, whether of their characters or their actions, or their sayings or their writings, we must ever bear in mind the views, the beliefs, the opinions, and the special circumstances of the time and the society in which they lived. Now, it is well known that in Elizabethan and Jacobean times opinion with regard to what I may call literary deception was very different from what it is at the present day when we at any rate affect much greater scrupulosity with regard to these matters. Such literary deceptions, which in these days would be condemned as " frauds," were, in those times, constantly

* See *Times Literary Supplement*, June 2, 1921. Article headed " Hamlet and History."

and habitually practised, and considered quite venial sins, if, indeed, they were looked upon as sins at all. That is a fact which should never be lost sight of when we are considering problems of authorship, or writings of dubious interpretation (such as some of Ben Jonson's, e.g.) in those long-gone and very different times.

Now, I am one of those who agree with the late Mr. Henry James, and with the present highly-distinguished French scholar and historian, Professor Abel Lefranc—I refer here to his negative views only—with regard to the authorship of the plays and poems of " Shakespeare." In my humble opinion (which, to be quite honest, I may say is not " humble " at all !), that the plays and poems of " Shakespeare " were not written by William Shakspere, the player who came from Stratford, is as certain as anything can be which is not susceptible of actual mathematical proof. Who then wrote the plays ? (Let us leave the poems on one side for the present). Well, that the work of many pens appears in the Folio of 1623 is surely indisputable. Few if any, of the " orthodox " would be found to deny it. There is little, if any, of " Shakespeare "—whoever he was—in the first part of *Henry VI*, and, surely, not much more in the second and third parts. Very little, if any part, of *The Taming of the Shrew* is " Shakespearean." The great majority of critics exclude *Titus* altogether. The work of pens other than the Shakespearean pen is to be found in *Pericles*, and *Timon*, and *Troilus and Cresssida*, and even in *Macbeth*. *Henry VIII*, though published as by " Shakespeare," was almost undoubtedly the

work of Fletcher and Massinger in collaboration.*
The list might be added to but it is unnecessary to
do so. I repeat, the work of many pens is to be
found in the Folio of 1623, but there is, of course,
one man whose work eclipses that of all the rest,
one man who stands pre-eminent and unrivalled,
towering high above the others ; one man of whom
it may be said, as of Marcellus of old, that *insignis
ingreditur, victorque viros supereminet omnes*. Find
that man, find the author of *Hamlet*, and *Lear*, and
Othello—to give but a few examples—and you will
have found the true " Shakespeare." But set your
hearts at rest ; you will never find him in the man
whose vulgar and banal life (in the course of which
not one—I do not say generous but—even respectable action can be discovered by all the researches
of his biographers) is to be read in the pages of
Halliwell-Phillipps and Sir Sidney Lee—the life
of which so little is known, and yet so much too
much !

Meantime it is amusing, or would be so if it were
not so lamentable, to see our solemn and entirely
self-satisfied Pundits and Mandarins of " Shakespearean " literature ever trying to see daylight
through the millstone of the Stratfordian faith ;
ever broaching some brand-new theory, and affecting
to find something in this Shakespearean literature
which nobody ever found before them, but which
as they fondly imagine, somehow, and in some way,
tends to support the old outworn Stratfordian
tradition. Perhaps some " prompt copy " of an

* See *Sidelights on Shakespeare* by H. Dugdale Sykes. (The Shakespeare Head Press, Stratford-upon-Avon. 1919.)

old Elizabethan drama is discovered. It is hailed with exultation as affording proof that plays in those times were printed from " prompt copies," and further cryptic arguments are adduced in support of the absurd theory that the Stratford player dashed off the plays of " Shakespeare," *currente calamo*, and handed them over to his fellow " deserving men," Heminge and Condell, and the rest, with " scarse a blot " upon them, and that the plays were printed from these precious " unblotted autographs." An old Manuscript Play is found. It is the work of several pens. In it are discovered three pages in an unknown hand. See now! Here is a hand " of the same class " as the " Shakespeare " (i.e., " Shakspere ") signatures! Why, it is Shakspere's own handwriting! Look at Shakspere's will—the will in which no book or manuscript is mentioned, but wherein are small bequests to Shakspere's fellow-players, those " deserving men " Burbage, and Heminge, and Condell, to buy them rings withal, and of the testator's sword, and parcel-gilt bowl, and " second-best bedstead "—and there you will find three words well and distinctly written in a firm hand—" By me William." Yes, and the " W " of " William " is so carefully written that it even has " the ornamental dot " under the curve of the right limb thereof! But why, then, are the signatures themselves such miserable, illegible scrawls? Oh, fools and blind! Cannot you see that player William in this case reversed the usual procedure ; that he intended to sign the last of the three pages of his Will first (" But *why*? "— " Oh, never mind *why*! ") ; that the poor man was *in extremis* (true he lived another month after signing, and his Will witnesses that he was " in perfect health and memorie, God be praysed ! " *Mais cela n'empêche pas*) ;   and that he made a tremendous effort, and wrote the words " By me William," in a fine distinct hand—" ornamental dot " and all !— and then collapsed utterly and could only make illiterate scrawls for his surname, and the other two signatures.   But these words, " By me William," are in the same handwriting as that of the " addition " to *Sir Thomas More* ! What ? You say they were manifestly written by the Law Scrivener ! *What ?* You say the handwriting of this " addition " differs manifestly and fundamentally from the handwriting of the " Shakspere " signatures (which, wretched scrawls as they are, differ profoundly one from the other), as anybody can see who does not happen to be a " paleographer " with an *idée fixe* ! What ? You say that ! Yah, fool ! Yah, fanatic ! What do *you* know about it, I should like to know !*

Such is all too frequently the language of the *soi-disant* "orthodox" to the poor " heretic " ; such are " the spurns that patient merit of the unworthy takes " !

Then we have a man—an " orthodox " wise-acre—who tells us that, without doubt, the " dark lady " of the Sonnets was Mistress Mary Fitton, and we are to subscribe to the belief that Mary Fitton, one of Elizabeth's Maids of Honour, had an intrigue with a common player—one " i' the statute ! " It is nothing to tell the people who have

---

* The theory that the handwriting of this " addition " to the play of *Sir Thomas More* is the same handwriting as that of the Shakspere signatures, is, I do not hesitate to say, one of the most absurd propositions ever advanced even in Shakespearean controversy.

made this wonderful discovery that Mary Fitton was *not* a " dark lady," but a *fair* lady, as her portraits at Arbury show. It is nothing to tell them that, though among the remarkable contemporaneous documents in the Muniment Room at Arbury there is much mention of Mary Fitton's *liaison* with that proud nobleman, Lord Pembroke, not a breath is to be discovered of any suggestion of her so degrading herself as to have an intrigue with " a man-player " —one who was a " rogue and vagabond " were it not for the licence of a great personage. No, all this goes for nothing when it is necessary somehow, by hook or by crook, to identify the Stratford player with the author of the Sonnets of " Shakespeare." *O miseras hominum mentes, O pectora cæca!*

Then yet another finds this " dark lady " in the person of the wife of an Oxford Inn Keeper, with whom, forsooth, player Shakspere had an intrigue, on his way from Stratford to London, or *vice versa*, and laborious investigations are undertaken, and many learned letters are written to the Press about this other imaginary " dark lady "—" that woman colour'd ill "*—and all the family history of the Davenants is exploited in this foolish quest. Then, again, another makes the discovery that William Shakspere, the Stratford player, had conceived a feeling of violent hatred against " Resolute John Florio," the translator of Montaigne (who was, by the way, so far as we know, a good worthy man), so he caricatures this hateful person in the hateful (!) character of Jack Falstaff—the Falstaff of *King Henry IV*! But we *don't* hate Jack Falstaff! On

*See *Sonnet* 144.

the contrary we all love old Jack Falstaff, in spite of his many faults and failings. We can't help loving him, for his unfailing good humour and his unrivalled wit! "Oh, that is nothing, nothing," says our critic from across the Atlantic—one Mr. Acheson of New York—who has made this grand discovery. "Will Shakspere of Stratford *hated* Florio, so he has lampooned him and ridiculed him in this hateful character of Falstaff! Of that there is no possible doubt. I am Sir Oracle, and when I speak let no dog bark! *"

And so I might go on to multiply the examples of this " Stratfordian " folly. And we, who see the absurdity of all this, are called " Fanatics ! " But what is " Fanaticism " ? It is the madness which possesses the worshippers at the shrine. These men have bowed themselves down at the traditional Stratfordian Shrine ; they have accepted without thinking the dogmas of the Stratfordian faith ; they are impervious to reasoning and to common sense ; they have surrendered their judgment ; " their eyes they have closed, lest at any time they should see with their eyes, and hear with their ears, and should understand with their hearts, and should be converted " to truth and reason. Verily, *these* are the real " fanatics."

Let me for a moment, before passing on, call

* It is only necessary to read the life of John Florio in the *Dict. of National Biography* or the *Encyc. Brit.* to appreciate the absurdity of this attempt to find him in Shakespeare's Falstaff. An almost equally silly attempt has been made by another sapient critic to identify him with Holofernes in *Love's Labour's Lost*. Now no two characters could be more dissimilar than those of Falstaff and Holofernes, yet Florio according to one wiseacre was the prototype of the former, and according to another wiseacre of the latter ! But there is no limit to the absurdities which are symptomatic of the *rabies Stratfordiana*.

attention to some words written by those distinguished " Shakespearean " critics Dr. Richard Garnett, and Dr. Edmund Gosse, in their *Illustrated English Literature*. They speak of " that knowledge of good society, and that easy and confident attitude towards mankind which appears in Shakespeare's plays *from the first*, and which are so unlike what might have been expected from *a Stratford rustic*. . . The first of his plays were undoubtedly the three early comedies, *Love's Labour's Lost*, *The Comedy of Errors*, and *The Two Gentlemen of Verona*, which must have appeared in 1590-1591, or perhaps in the latter year only. The question of priority among them is hard to settle, but we may concur with Mr. [now Sir Sidney] Lee in awarding precedence to *Love's Labour's Lost*. All three indicate that the runaway Stratford youth had, within five or six years, made himself the perfect gentleman, master of the manners and language of the best society of his day, and able to hold his own with any contemporary writer."*

Now this miraculous " runaway Stratford youth," came to London " a Stratford rustic," in the year 1587,† and, according to his biographers, being a penniless adventurer, had to seek for a living in " very mean employments," as Dr. Johnson says, whether as horse-holder, or " call boy," or " super " on the stage, or what you will. His parents were entirely illiterate, and he left his two daughters in

---

* *English Literature*. An Illustrated Record (1903), pp. 199, 200, 202. Italics mine.

† So says that distinguished Shakespearean scholar, Mr. Fleay, who points out that in the previous year the theatres were closed owing to the plague.

the same darkness of ignorance. We may assume that he had attended for a few years at the " Free School " at Stratford (as Rowe, his earliest biographer, calls it), although there is really no evidence in support of that assumption, but it is admitted even by the most zealous and orthodox Stratfordians that he " had received only an imperfect education."*

But I will not again recapitulate the facts (real or supposed) of this mean and vulgar life. Let the reader, I say again, study it in the pages of Halliwell-Phillipps, and Sir Sidney Lee.†

And now let us consider for a moment hat extraordinary play, *Love's Labour's Lost*, which, as we have seen, " appeared " in 1590 or 1591, according to Messrs. Garnett and Gosse, but of which Mr. Fleay writes: " The date of the original production cannot well be put later than 1589." It was, as the " authorities " are all agreed, Shakespeare's first drama, and it is remarkable for this fact, among other things, that unlike other Shakespearean plays it is not an old play re-written, nor is the plot taken from some other writer. The plot of *Love's Labour's Lost* is an original one.

And now let us see what Professor Lefranc, who has made a very special study of this play, has to tell us about it, premising that I do not cite his remarks as " authoritative," but merely as a clear statement of the facts of the case by one who has exceptional knowledge of the history of the time in which the action of the play is supposed to take place.

---

*Sir E. Maunde Thompson, in *Shakespeare's Handwriting*, p. 26.

†So far, that is, as Sir Sidney's *Life of Shakespeare* is, or purports to be, biographical, and setting aside the " fanciful might-have-beens."

" Everybody knows," he writes, " that the scene of this very original comedy is laid at the Court of Navarre, at a date nearly contemporaneous with the play, when Henri de Bourbon was the reigning sovereign of this little kingdom, before he became Henri IV of France. . . . That the author of *Love's Labour's Lost* knew and had visited the Court of Navarre is at once obvious to anyone who will study the play without any preconceived hypothesis and who takes the trouble to learn something about the history of this little Kingdom of Nérac. . . All the explanations which have been given of this play, the first of the Shakespearean dramas, in order to bolster up the theory of its composition by Shakspere the player at the very outset of his career as a playwright, as also every element of the comedy itself, and every known incident in the life of the Stratford player, prove the impossibility of his being the author of it. All these theories and hypotheses put forward during the last 120 years are of such total improbability, indeed of such miserable tenuity, that some day people will wonder how they could possibly find acceptance for so long."

M. Lefranc cites Montegut, a French Shakespearean scholar and a critic of noted insight and perspicacity, who writes: " It is extraordinary to see how Shakespeare is faithful even in the most minute details to historical truth and to local colour," and he proceeds to demonstrate that many allusions in this wonderful play of *Love's Labour's Lost* cannot be properly understood or appreciated without reference to the memoirs of the celebrated Marguerite de Valois, who is herself the " Princess

INTRODUCTORY

of France " of the comedy (in the original edition called " The Queen "*), who comes with her suite to visit Henri at his Court of Nérac.   The Princess of France, then, was originally Queen Marguerite of Navarre, and this comedy represents her as coming to rejoin her husband at Nérac to endeavour to regain his love, and to settle many questions relative to her dowry of Aquitaine.   That this journey actually took place, that Marguerite paid a long visit to the Court of Navarre where a series of entertainments were held in her honour, and that the question of her dowry in Aquitaine was then discussed at length is established by the Memoirs of Marguerite de Valois.†   The author, then, had in his mind events of contemporaneous history which had taken place at the Court of Navarre, and with which he appears to have been personally familiar.   The memoirs, too, throw light on several passages of the drama which would be obscure without them. Take (e.g.) Act II, Sc. 1, where Biron asks Rosaline, " Did not I dance with you at Brabant once ? " Here we have an allusion to the visit of Marguerite to Spain 1577, of which a full account is given in her Memoirs, where she tells of balls at Mons, Namur, and Liege, all in a country which was at that time constantly spoken of as Brabant. Again, in Act V, Sc. 2, there is an obscure allusion, which seems to be satisfactorily explained by a reference to the story of the unfortunate Hélène de Tournon,

* She so appears in the Quarto, and also in the Folio in certain places (II. 1 and IV. 1, e.g.) where, as in other passages, the play seems to have been imperfectly revised.

† Boyet in the play (II. 1) calls upon the Princess (or Queen) to reflect that her mission to Navarre was to raise a claim " of no less weight than Aquitaine, a dowry for a Queen."

related by Marguerite in her Memoirs. Further, in Act V, Sc. 2, we have an allusion to the manner in which Henri of Navarre, the " Vert Galant," wrote, prepared, and sealed his love letters, as though the author was familiar with the amorous King's poetical letter addressed by him to the " Charmante Gabrielle " d'Estrés ; while the circumstances described in Act I, Sc. 1, are explained in the light of fact by a letter from Cobham to Walsingham dated from Paris in June, 1583.

But it would take far too much time to dilate further upon this, the first of the Shakespearean plays. I can only refer my readers, for further light, to Professor Lefranc's work *Sous le Masque de William Shakespeare.**

Yet we are required to believe—nay, we are " fanatics " if we do not believe—that this extraordinary play was composed by the " Stratford rustic " some two years after he had " run away " from Stratford, and, further, that he composed two other remarkable comedies, *The Comedy of Errors*, and *The Two Gentlemen of Verona*, just about the same time ! Verily this is a faith which does not remove mountains, but simply swallows them whole—a faith which appears to me more worthy of Bedlam than of the intelligence of rational human beings. On the other hand, there is no difficulty whatever in believing that this unique play—which shows that the author of it was not only a " perfect gentleman, master of the manners and language of the best society of the day," but also one familiar with the doings, and " happenings " and amusements

---

* Vol. II, ch. 7.

INTRODUCTORY

and *entourage* of the Court of Henri of Navarre at Nérac on the occasion of the visit of Marguerite de Valois to that Court—was written by a man who lived and moved in a very different sphere of society from that in which Shakspere of Stratford lived and moved, but who was desirous of concealing his identity as a playwright under a convenient mask-name.

Yet, as M. Lefranc truly says, " L'hétérodoxie dans ce domaine [the " Shakespearean " authorship to wit] a paru jusqu'à présent aux maîtres des universités et aux érudits, une opinion de mauvais goût, temeraire et malséante, dont la science patentée n'avait pas à s'occuper, sauf pour la condamner."* But he continues—I will now translate—" I am convinced that every one who has preserved an independent opinion concerning the Shakespeare problem will recognise that the old positions of the traditional doctrine can no longer be maintained. . . . The laws of psychology, and, what is more, of simple common sense, ought to banish for ever the absurd theory which would have us believe in an incomparable writer whose life was absolutely out of harmony with the marvellous works which appeared in his name. It is time to take decisive action against that immense error, and against the incredible *naiveté* upon which it rests."

" Simple common sense." Aye, but when I spoke not long ago to a well-known writer, who is a Stratfordian *enragé*, of " common sense " in this matter, what was his reply ? " *Oh, damn common*

---

* *Sous le Masque*, vol. I, 21. He might, I think, have included certain editors of newspapers and magazines in his statement, though not always " *érudits*."

sense ! "—a characteristic interjection which might well be adopted as the motto of all the " Stratfordian " highbrows of the present day.

But, adds Professor Lefranc, " If many still refuse to admit the existence of a Shakespeare problem, yet the time is at hand when nobody will any longer venture to deny it, unless he is prepared at the same time to deny all the evidence in the case. It is clear that a new era of Shakespearean study has recently presented itself. Scepticism with regard to the Stratford man is spreading in spite of the resistance of the multifarious defenders of the old tradition. A number of beliefs, accepted for many years as dogmas, are disappearing every day. The rock of credulity is crumbling away. The Stratfordians will, sooner or later, be reduced, under the pressure of a more enlightened public opinion, to change their tactics and modify the assumptions of their creed. In truth, speaking generally, the best-established reproach to which the learned men who have concerned themselves with Shakespeare, according to the rules of Stratfordian orthodoxy, have laid themselves open, is not so much that they have maintained the traditional doctrine with regard to the poet-actor, but rather that in the face of the innumerable enigmas which are involved in the history of his life, and his [supposed] works, and even of the text of those works, they have never had the candour to admit even the existence of all these obscure problems. At every step in Shakespearean study these difficulties and incoherences are encountered, but these learned men affect ·not to see them. . . . Truly, in view of such superb assurance, the lay reader could never imagine the existence of all the gratuitous assumptions, the naïve assertions, the inadmissible interpretations that are to be found in the works of these gentlemen, which the public have been accustomed to accept as infallible authorities. Yet, even the most famous and the most admired amongst them would have to yield to an investigation conducted according to the simple rules of the art of reasoning, that is to say of sound common sense. The hour has come when the representatives of the ' Shakespearean ' dogma will have to change their attitude. They will have to renounce both their silence and their credulity. Above all, they will have to admit the necessity of inquiries, and discussions hostile to their creed, to make a *tabula rasa* of many points, and to take in hand once more the investigation thereof *ab imis fundamentis*, resolutely putting away those prejudices which have so long blinded them to the truth."

So writes Professor Abel Lefranc, with much more to the same purport and effect, and, in my judgment, he writes both wisely and well. But if he really believes that our hidebound Pundits and Mandarins of the Stratfordian faith will ever "put away those prejudices which have so long blinded them to the truth," and give impartial consideration to the facts of the Shakespeare Problem in the light of reason and "commonsense," I fear me he reckons without his host and is destined to be very sadly undeceived.*

* M. Abel Lefranc, it may be mentioned, is *Professeur au Collège de France*, and one of our highest authorities on Rabelais and the period of the Renaissance, not to mention Moliére, and other historical periods. " But, surely, we need not go to a Frenchman for enlightenment on our

We are brought back, however, to the question: Who, then, is the real " Shakespeare " ? That is a question which I have never attempted to answer. It has been quite sufficient for me to confine my arguments to the negative side of the Shakespeare Problem. The positive, or constructive side I have hitherto been content to leave to others.

Now, there is a large number of persons, many of them rational and intelligent men and women, of quite sound mind and understanding, who believe that the real " Shakespeare " is to be found in the person of Francis Bacon. But there are " Baconians and Baconians." There are the wild Baconians who find Bacon everywhere, but especially in ciphers, cryptograms, anagrams, acrostics, and in all sorts of occult figures and emblems*—those who believe amongst other things, that Bacon was the son of Queen Elizabeth, that he lived in philosophic concealment many years after the date usually assigned as that of his death, that he wrote prac-

great English poet ! " wrote a British commentator in the Press the other day—a most characteristic utterance, and superbly illustrative of the insular conceit which no *entente cordiale* seems to have the power to dissipate. But is it not highly probable that a French scholar, applying himself to the study of the Shakespeare Problem with an impartial mind, with no innate or national prejudices to obscure his vision, being himself an enthusiastic worshipper at the shrine of Shakespeare, the poet and dramatist, might be able to throw light upon many things which are " beyond the skyline " of those who have grown up in the school of an old and unquestioned tradition to which they cling as though it were part and parcel of the British constitution, and, as it were, a necessary ingredient of the national glory ?

* I am, I need scarcely say, very far from denying the possible existence of ciphers, cryptograms, and anagrams, whether in " Shakespeare's " plays and poems or in other literature of that day. It is known that such things were frequently made use of by writers of the sixteenth and early seventeenth centuries. Bacon himself gives us an example of the biliteral cipher, and it is known that he often employed such cryptic methods of writing. It is none the less true that the search for these things by " Baconian " enthusiasts of the present day has fre-quently led to very distressing results, for " that way madness lies."

tically all the English literature worthy of that name of the Elizabethan and Jacobean period, and that he hid his " Shakespearean " manuscripts in the mud of the River Wye or some other equally inappropriate and ridiculous place, where no sane man would ever dream of looking for them.

The wild and unrestrained " Baconians " have, undoubtedly, done great injury to the cause which they desire to advocate ; and not only have they injured that cause, but they have greatly prejudiced the discussion of the Shakespeare Problem as a whole. For in such cases we are all liable to be " tarred by the same brush," and the sanest of " Anti-Stratfordian " reasoners has, unfortunately, not escaped the back-wash of the ridicule which these eccentrics have brought upon themselves.

There are, however, " Baconians " of another class—the sane " Baconians " who are content to argue the matter—and some of them have argued it with great knowledge and ability—in the calm light of reason and common sense. Of these one of the sanest and ablest was my friend the late Edward Walter Smithson, whose little book *Shakespeare—Bacon. An Essay*,* published anonymously some three and twenty years ago, attracted no little attention, and did much to help the cause in support of which it was written. He published, however, nothing more on the subject till 1913, in November of which year there appeared in *The Nineteenth Century* an article from his pen entitled " Ben Jonson's Pious Fraud." The greater part of this article I have quoted by way of preface to his essay

* Swan Sonnenschein & Co., 1899.

now published on Jonson's Masque of *Time Vindicated*,* and it may be as well to cite the commencement of it at this place :

The writer is one of those persons who consider it highly probable that Shakespeare was at first a mere pen-name of Bacon's, and regard Shakspere, Shaxper, or Shayksper— easily mistaken for Shakespeare—as the usual patronymic from birth to death of an illiterate actor : he thinks, moreover, that there must have been some sort of understanding between the poet and the actor (resembling perhaps that between Aristophanes and the actor Callistratus), and conjectures that it may have covered proprietary rights or shares in theatrical ventures.

When and how I came by such views can be of little or no interest to anyone but myself. To prevent misconception, however, it may be well to explain that my conversion dates from 1884-5. An essay of mine (*Shakespeare-Bacon*, Sonnenschein, 1900)† belonging in substance to 1885, would have been published long before the date of actual publication but for the appearance of a portent called the *Great Cryptogram*, which put me out of love with the subject. My earliest suspicions were suggested not by heretics—Mr. W. H. Smith, Lord Campbell, Lord Penzance, and the rest—whose opinions were absolutely unknown to me, but, if memory serve, by Mr. Halliwell-Phillipps and the New Shakspere Society (of which I must have been an early member). Since 1885, I have tried to keep in touch with what orthodoxy has had to say for itself, and against us. Some of our opponents regard Ben Jonson as their prophet. To him they fly for counsel and comfort. They throw his sayings at our heads whenever they get a chance. In the index to Mr. Lang's *Shakespeare-Bacon and the Great Unknown* (1912) Ben Jonson's name takes up more space than even Shakespeare's. According to Mr. Lang " it is easy to prove that Will (i.e. the Stratford man) was recognised as the author by Ben Jonson." If this were true there would be no Shakespeare question at all, none at least so far as I am concerned. But it is not true. Ben Jonson—whose *Works* ought to be familiar to all students of Shakespeare—is in fact what lawyers would call a difficult witness, and to assert that he is on the side of orthodoxy is simply to beg the question.‡

* This Masque, also called " The Prince's Masque," forms the subject of two chapters (VI and VII) in Mr. Smithson's book, *Shakespeare—Bacon*.

† The title-page bears date 1899. [G. G.]

‡ I may be allowed to refer to my booklet, *Ben Jonson and Shakespeare* (Cecil Palmer, 1921). [G. G.]

INTRODUCTORY

Some of Mr. Lang's admirers will have it that he has crushed Mr. G. G. Greenwood much as a motor-car might crumple up a bicycle. But a reading of Mr. Lang's book leaves me in doubt whether Mr. Greenwood's main contentions (*The Shakespeare Problem Restated*) are anywhere shaken, and I am not likely to be very strongly biassed in Mr. Greenwood's favour, seeing that he ostentatiously disclaims being a Baconian. Mr. Greenwood indeed may be said to have quitted Stratford for good and travelled a great many miles. Where he pulls up it is not easy to say, but he does pull up somewhere—perhaps where the rainbow ends. Mr. Lang, though he refrains from imputing imbecility to Mr. Greenwood, is apparently unable to be quite so lenient to Baconians. He explains, or would like to explain, the Baconian views of Lord Penzance and Judge Webb as partly due to senile decay. How he accounts for the views of Lord Campbell,* Mr. George Bidder, Q.C., and others of less note does not appear. When an unfamiliar theory happens to be at grips with a popular one, the habit of thinking and calling an opponent infatuated or not more than half mad is easily caught. Bacon did not escape it, but he took care to give it a turn which saved it from mere *brutalité*. In his day two notable theories were at loggerheads, the Ptolemaic and the Copernican, with Galileo for the Copernican Achilles. Convinced that the Sun moved round the Earth, Bacon smiled at his opponents for doubting the immovability of our planet and dubbed them " car-men," " terrae aurigas," chauffeurs, in other words. No other student of *The Advancement of Learning* (1605), written be it remembered when Bacon was fully mature, will be surprised at this. Bacon avowedly took " all knowledge for his province," and *The Advancement* is a comprehensible survey of that province—as Bacon understood it. Of mathematics he probably knew little or nothing. It is an open question whether Induction owes anything to the *Novum Organum*. His acquaintance with the phenomena of nature (as distinct from human nature) was derived for the most part from poets and men of letters. More significant still, his splendid natural gifts were not adapted to scientific research. His true province in short was literature, above all, poetry. And here it may not be amiss to note (1) that John Dryden's appreciation of Shakespeare—in whom, says J. D., are to be found " all arts and sciences, all moral and natural philosophy "—coincides as closely as may be with the traditional estimate of Bacon, and (2) that Shakespeare seems to have been of one mind with Bacon upon the motion of the Sun round the Earth.

With the tons of printed matter on the Baconian side, my

---

* But Lord Campbell cannot be quoted as a ' Baconian." [G. G.]

acquaintance has always been of the smallest. In a recent pamphlet by Sir E. Durning Lawrence, that gentleman with the aid of a newspaper called *The Tailor and Cutter* labours the point, already sufficiently obvious, that the figure which does duty as frontispiece to the first folio of Shakespeare must have been meant for a caricature.

What the Shakespeare theory is needs no telling. It is developed in *Biographies*, *Lives*, and so forth, within the reach of every one.

The Bacon theory on the other hand is still in the rough. "You may well say that," an opponent exclaims. "You, Baconians, differ among yourselves almost as widely as you differ from us. With some of you it is an article of faith that Bacon looked for fame (poetical) to after ages, and took unheard-of pains to secure it. Baconians who hunt for ciphers, key-numbers and so forth, not only in books, but even under the river Wye belong to this class. You on the contrary have convinced yourself, I know not how, that Bacon intended his secret to die with him. What are we to do ? How can we help thinking that there is no such thing as a passably authentic Baconian theory ?" My acquaintance with Baconians, I reply, is far too limited to justify any important attempt at sketching an authoritative theory. My object is less ambitious. It is to set down, as briefly and simply as possible, by way of introduction to Ben Jonson, certain probable constituents of a reasonable Baconian theory.

(*a*) Shakespeare was a pseudonym adopted by Bacon to mask his personality whenever he created or " made " for the stage.

(*b*) The date at which Bacon gave up writing for public theatres coincided pretty nearly with the beginning of his rise to high place in the State.

(*c*) By the year 1623 (if not earlier) Bacon's friends and admirers must have become very uneasy about the fate of his still unpublished plays. These plays had long been hidden away from the public eye. What if the veil should never be lifted ? Lest that should happen, publication, and the sooner the better, must have been eagerly desired by all lovers of literature. The conditions were not unpromising. Softened by misfortune, Bacon would be open to entreaty, and publication just then would put it in the power of influential friends to minister with perfect delicacy to the more urgent needs of the fallen man, " old, weak, ruined, in want, a very subject of pity." Provided that his true name could be for ever kept from contact with the " family " of her who had once been his " mistress,"*

*See Jonson's censure of Poetry in his day, for being " a meane Mistresse to such as have wholly addicted themselves to her ; or given their his consent or rather acquiescence might be hoped for. Values it is true, literary and poetical values especially, were no longer what they had been in the days of the late Queen. But a parent's affection for the offspring of his brain is never perhaps wholly uprooted. Even so, the task was one for a master of literary craft. But the thing had to be done and that quickly, if it was to be of any use to the great man who, to quote Jonson's *Discoveries*, had " filled up all numbers, and performed that in our tongue which may be compar'd or preferr'd either to insolent Greece or haughty Rome." No considerable help was to be looked for from Bacon himself. The lie downright was to be avoided if possible ; but the motive being perfectly clean, economy of truth and suggestion of untruth were neither of them barred. The pseudonym was ready to hand, and the players Heminge and Condell were not likely to deny their names to any prefatory matter whatever which the editor might think fit to invent.

(*d*) Among the notable persons who openly interested themselves in the publication of the First Folio were the Earl of Pembroke, the Earl of Montgomery, and Ben Jonson. But it is safe to say that they were not the only promoters of the undertaking, and in my opinion King James (himself a poet in days gone by), Prince Charles, and some *alter ego* of Bacon's (possibly Sir T. Mathews) were of the number.

(*e*) A private printing press may have been among the tools habitually employed by the author. Heminge and Condell in the First Folio are made to say : " We have scarce received from him (Shakespeare) a blot in his papers." As an allusion to the use of a press this statement would pass muster.* It occurs in the prefatory matter, thoroughly Jonsonian, which seems to have served as receptacle for what he preferred to put upon other shoulders than his own.

(*f*) As for Shakspere—the man who emerged from and returned to Stratford somehow and somewhen—he while he lived was a nobody outside Stratford, and by the year 1622 must have been almost forgotten even there, except as a good

names up to her family. They who have but saluted her on the by . . . she hath done much for, and advanced in the way of their own professions, both the *Law* and the *Gospel*, beyond all they could have hoped without her favour." This means, I take it, that Jonson had in his eye Bacon and others as striking examples of Poetry's generosity, and himself a shining illustration of her meanness. As for the prosperous burgher of Stratford, he was not in the picture, for Jonson was treating of poets. [Original Note.]

* But surely this statement, put into the mouths of the players by the author of the Folio preface, could not have referred to *printed* matter? If the players did indeed, receive papers with " scarce a blot " they were, doubtless, fair copies. [G. G.]

sort of fellow who, having made money in London, had invested it in Stratford with a view to enjoying the congenial society of its artless natives. His *Apotheosis* probably began with the publication of Jonson's own Ode.

" Guesswork ! " exclaims one. " Mere figments of the brain !" says another. Well, where is the theory which does not consist of such material ? Take away from any orthodox life-story of Shakspere all figments of somebody's brain, and what remains ? According to Professor Saintsbury, " almost all the received stuff of his life-story is shreds and patches of tradition, if not positive dream-work."

Here it becomes necessary to say a word in explanation of the present work. The late Edward Smithson left by his Will a sum of money to myself and a friend who prefers to remain anonymous, with the suggestion that it might be made use of in the endeavour to ascertain—to use his own words—" the true parentage of Shakespeare (not Shakspere)," meaning thereby, as there can be no doubt, that such sum might be employed, if thought well—for there was no definite trust attached to it—in furtherance of the quest of the true " Shakespeare," whether he might be found in Francis Bacon (as he himself thought was the case) or in some other writer of the period in question. Moreover, he had left in type certain " Baconian " essays, which, although he gave no specific directions to that effect, it was known that he desired to be published as his last words on a matter in which he was so deeply interested, and these, at the request of his wife who survives him, I have supervised and prepared for publication. Here a difficulty presented itself. Some of these essays deal, to a certain extent, with the same subject matter, and, consequently, the reader will find in them a certain amount of repetition. At first I thought it might be possible to avoid this by collating the various manuscripts, and fusing them together, as it were, into one volume. It soon became apparent, however, that such " fusion " would lead to " confusion," and would be detrimental to Mr. Smithson's work. I trust, therefore, that the recurrence of various arguments, or sentiments, in the following essays, will meet with generous toleration on the part of the reader. After all, a certain amount of repetition is, sometimes, likely to do more good than harm. The famous Mr. Justice Maule, while still at the Bar, was once arguing a case before three Judges, one of whom, finding the distinguished counsel somewhat prolix on this occasion, and inclined to repeat his arguments, exclaimed testily : " Really, Mr. Maule, that is the third time you have made that observation ! " " Well," replied Maule, quite imperturbably, " there are *three* of your Lordships ! " To repeat an argument once for each Judge on the Bench was, then, in this great advocate's opinion, quite a right, proper, and useful thing to do. I am in hopes, therefore, that there may be the same justification for a considerable amount of repetition in the case now presented to a court—that of the reading public—which, it is hoped, may consist of many more Judges than those addressed by Mr. Justice Maule.

I would make this further observation with regard to Edward Smithson's Essays, though perhaps it is hardly necessary to make it. Although it has been a pleasure to me to edit them, so far as they required editing at all, I have, of course, no responsibility for the arguments or the opinions expressed in them. Mr. Smithson, in the passage I have quoted above from his article in *The Nineteenth Century*, says that I " ostentatiously disclaim being a Baconian." I am sorry if that disclaimer was made " ostentatiously," but speaking now, after the lapse of many years, and I trust without a shred of " ostentation "—which, certainly, would be very much out of place—I must say that I am still unwilling to label myself as a " Baconian." It was, I think, Professor Huxley who said that, if asked whether he believed that there were inhabitants in Mars, his reply would be that he neither believed nor disbelieved. He did not know. This is the " agnostic " position in which I find myself with regard to the hypothesis that Bacon is the true Shakespeare. I really do not know. Nevertheless, an astronomer who had adopted Professor Huxley's position concerning the possible existence of inhabitants in Mars, might without prejudice to that agnostic position, find himself impelled to set forth certain arguments which seemed to him to tell in favour of such a possibility. In the same way it occurred to me some years ago to write certain essays on the Baconian side of the case, two of which I now venture to publish as a sequel to those of Mr. Smithson's authorship. I recognise that there is much that may quite fairly and reasonably be urged in favour of the Baconian case. Merely to ridicule that case appears to me to be indicative of folly rather than wisdom on the part of those who adopt such an attitude. Nevertheless, when all is said and done, I am far from thinking that the Baconian authorship of any of the plays or poems published in the name of " Shakespeare " has been actually proved. That Francis Bacon had, at any rate, something to do with the production of some of these plays and poems is, at least, a very plausible hypothesis. As Professor Lefranc writes, " Que l'auteur du théâtre Shakespearien ait été en rapport avec Francis Bacon, c'est ce que nous avons toujours été porté à admettre pour bien des raisons,"* and in support of that hypothesis I may be said to hold a brief *pro hâc vice* in the two " Baconian " Essays which I now venture to publish. But that is all. I endeavour to keep an open mind upon this, as upon many other doubtful questions. Professor Lefranc himself has shown, with great learning and conspicuous ability, that a strong case can be made in favour of William Stanley, Sixth Earl of Derby, as the author of some, at any rate, of the " Shakespearean " plays, and more especially of that extraordinary play *Love's Labour's Lost*.† But the constructive side of the " Shakespeare Problem " I must be content to leave to younger and abler men, and such as have much more time to devote to it than I have. With regard, however, to " the man from Stratford," as Mr. Henry James styles him, or the " Stratford rustic," as Messrs. Garnett and Gosse do not hesitate to characterize him, *his* supposed authorship may, and, indeed, must be, set aside as one of the greatest and most unfortunate of the many delusions which have, from

---

* See *Sous le Masque de Shakespeare*. Vol. I, p. 130.

† As for the claims of Edward de Vere, 17th Earl of Oxford, see *"Shakespeare" Identified*, by J. Thomas Looney (Cecil Palmer, 1920).

time to time, imposed themselves upon a credulous and " patient world."*

I cannot conclude this note without a brief reference to two articles which have lately appeared in the *Quarterly Review* (October, 1921, and January, 1922), under the heading of " Recent Shakespearean Research," by Mr. C. R. Haines. I can find little or nothing that can be recalled " recent " in them unless we give a quite unwonted extension to the meaning of that word. Mr. Haines even includes such *vieux jeu* as the Plume MSS. in his " recent " Shakespearean Research, but they certainly contain some very remarkable statements. I will, however, here content myself by quoting the following letter which I sent to the *Nation and Athenæum* after reading the first of these articles, and which appeared in that paper on November 26th, last :

* With reference to the " Baconian " theory I must here quote words recently written by one who bears a highly distinguished name in the ranks of literature. Mr. George Moore, writing in reply to a criticism by Mr. Gosse, published in the *Sunday Times*, thus expresses his opinion upon that question : " Some of Shakespeare's finest plays were not only revised, but remoulded ; ' Hamlet ' is one of these, and it is not an exaggeration to say that its revisions were spread over at least twenty years ; and I thought when I wrote the little booklet, ' Fragments from Héloïse and Abélard,' that the text of ' Othello ' in the Folio contained 160 lines that are not to be found in the quarto, and I think so still ; 160 lines were added between the publication of the quarto [in 1622] and the folio [1623], and these lines cannot be attributed to any other hand but the author's ; they are among the best in the play, and among them will be found lines dear to all who hold the belief that Bacon and not the mummer was the author of the plays :

> Like the Pontic Sea
> Whose icy current and compulsive course
> Ne'er feels retiring ebb, but keeps due on
> To the Propontic and the Helespont."

See the *Sunday Times*, August 28, 1921. With reference to the 160 new lines added in the folio version of *Othello* and which " cannot be attributed to any other hand but the author's," it will be remembered that William Shakspere of Stratford died some six years before the publication of the quarto of 1622. (See *Is there a Shakespeare Problem ?* p. 443 *et seq.*)

INTRODUCTORY

" RECENT SHAKESPEAREAN RESEARCH."

Sir,—In an article under the above heading in the October number of the *Quarterly Review*, Mr. C. R. Haines writes (p. 229) : " There cannot be the smallest doubt that Shakespeare [i.e., William Shakspere, of Stratford] was possessed of books at his death. One of these, *with his undoubted signature* [my italics], ' W. Sh^r.' is still extant in the Bodleian Library. . . . A second, Florio's version of Montaigne (1603), bears the signature ' Wilm Shakspere,' which is with some reason regarded as genuine."

Now Sir Edward Maunde Thompson, who, I believe, is generally considered our foremost " paleographer," has told us that the " Florio's Montaigne " signature is an " undoubted forgery " (I have in my possession a letter of his addressed from the British Museum in 1904 to the late Sir Herbert Tree, and kindly forwarded by the latter to me, in which Sir Edward so states) ; and the same high authority writes in " Shakespeare's England " (Vol. I, p. 308, n.) : " Nor is it possible to give a higher character to the signature, ' W^m Sh^e.' (not ' W. Sh^r,' as Mr. Haines prints it) in the Aldine Ovid's ' Metamorphoses,' 1502, in the Bodleian Library."

How in the face of this Mr. C. R. Haines can assert that the book referred to, in the Bodleian Library, bears Shakespeare's " undoubted signature," or that the " Florio" signature is with reason regarded as genuine, I am quite unable to understand.

A further question is suggested by the following passage in Mr. Haines's article. Alluding to the suit of " Belott *v.* Mountjoy," he writes : " From this suit we also learn an interesting by-fact, namely, that Belott and his wife, after quitting the Mountjoys, lived in the house of George Wilkins, the playwright, who had the honour of collaborating with Shakespeare in 'Pericles,' and possibly in 'Timon.'" Here I would ask what particle of evidence is there that the "George Wilkins, Victualler," mentioned in the action, was George Wilkins the pamphleteer and hack-dramatist ? It is true Professor Wallace has told us that, although " we have known nothing about Wilkins personally before," he thinks that " more than one reader with a livelier critical interest in these [Shakespearean] plays may be able to *smell the victualler* " (*Harper's Magazine*, March, 1910, p. 509) ; but, really, we can hardly be expected to put implicit confidence in the deductions of Dr. Wallace's olfactory organ. What warrant, then, has Mr. Haines to characterize as a " fact " that which is only guess-work and assumption ? For my part, I can no more " smell the victualler " in the author of " The Miseries of Inforst Marriage " than I can "smell " (as did Professor Wallace) the French official Herald in Mountjoy of Muggle Street !

One more question and I have done, though many more occur to me. Mr. Haines invites our attention to " The Plume MSS., which gave us the only glimpse of John Shakespeare at his home, cracking jests with his famous son " (p. 241). May I respectfully ask him if it is not the fact that this pleasant picture of John Shakespeare rests upon the (alleged) statement of Sir John Mennes, and that Sir John

INTRODUCTORY

Mennes was born on March 1st, 1599, whereas John Shakespeare died in September, 1601, so that the infant Mennes must, presumably, have been taken from his cradle in Kent, in his nurse's arms, for the purpose of interviewing that " merry-cheeked old man," of which interview he made a record from memory when he had learnt to write ?

I trust Mr. Haines will enlighten a perplexed inquirer as to these matters in the second article, which, as I gather, he is to contribute to the *Quarterly Review* on the results of " Recent Shakespearean Research."—Yours, &c.,

GEORGE GREENWOOD.

I turned, therefore, with some interest to Mr. Haines's second article, but, alas, I found no enlightenment therein. He has treated my questions with a very discreet silence. Well, no doubt " silence is golden "—in some cases. But such is " Shakespearean " criticism at the present day, of which these articles are a very instructive and characteristic specimen. I am aware, of course, that if I were to offer a paper in reply to them, however conclusive that reply might be, and even if it were quite up to the literary standard of the *Review* in question, it would be at once returned to me by the editor—if not consigned to the " W.P.B."—for the all-sufficient reason that the writer is guilty of vile and intolerable heresy (to wit that he shares the conviction of the late Henry James—and many others alive and dead—that the author of *Hamlet* and *Lear* and *Othello* was actually a well-educated man, of high position, and the representative of the highest culture of his day), and is therefore *taboo* to the editors of all decent journals. *Id sane intolerandum!* Indeed, with the exception of the editor of the *National Review*—to whom the thanks of all un-prejudiced and liberal-minded men are most justly due—I know of no editor of an English quarterly or monthly magazine, since the lamented death of Mr. Wray Skilbeck, who does not maintain this boycott as though it were a matter of moral obligation, just as but a few years since they boycotted the Free-thinker and the Rationalist. They freely open their columns to attacks upon the " Anti-Stratfordian," but on no account must he be allowed to reply.

Whether such an attitude redounds to the credit of English literature it is not for me, a " heretic," to say. I would only venture to refer the reader to the observations of Professor Abel Lefranc—a scholar and critic of European reputation—upon this matter, in whose judgment it seems that such an attitude with regard to an extremely interesting literary problem is not only absurdly prejudiced and narrow-minded, but one which—I tremble as I say it—makes some of our literary highbrows not a little ridiculous in the eyes of men of common sense and unfettered judgment.*　　　　G. G.

* In the *Fortnightly Review* of January, 1922, Mr. W. Bayley Kempling gravely informs us that Shakespeare bestowed the name of " Mountjoy " on the French Herald in *Henry V.* in honour of the " tire-maker " of that name with whom player Shakespeare lodged for a time in Magwell (i.e., Monkwell) Street, thereby repeating the preposterous error of Dr. Wallace (often exposed by the present writer amongst others) who wrote in ignorance of the fact that " Mountjoy King at Arms " was the official name of a French Herald who, as Holinshed informs us, made his appearance at Agincourt ! Had Mr. Kempling condescended to read an " heretical " author he might have been saved from this absurd mistake.

THE MASQUE OF " TIME
VINDICATED "

THE MASQUE OF "TIME VINDICATED"*

The following extract from Mr. Smithson's Article in *The Nineteenth Century* of November 1913, headed "Ben Jonson's Pious Fraud," may well stand as a preface to his now published Essay on Jonson's Masque of *Time Vindicated*, which was written by him in the year 1919. The reader may also be referred to Chapters VI and VII of his *Shakespeare-Bacon*, published in 1899.

It is odd that we Baconians, differing as we do from our opponents in so many points, should agree with them so entirely on one—the supreme importance of the testimony of Ben Jonson. This paper is mainly concerned with two of his utterances, the Ode in the First Folio, and the *Prince's Masque*. Both the one and the other belong in point of composition to the same period, 1622-3. We will begin with the *Masque* completed no doubt a few months earlier than the Ode. In my opinion they were vital parts of one great scheme of which Bacon, i.e., Bacon-Shakespeare, was the subject.

The genesis of the *Prince's Masque* was probably on this wise : assuming that Bacon was bent on disowning his plays, the publication of them, however generous in intention, could at best be only a left-handed compliment to him. Consequently if the scheme was to yield any true satisfaction to its originators (or any suitable consolation to Bacon regarded as the victim of malicious if not disloyal persecution), it would have to give scope for some direct (*ad virum*) expression, in their own persons

* This Essay was written by Mr. Smithson in 1919-20.

if possible, of love and admiration for their hero. A prince brought up in the court of James the First would be sure to decide that a Masque was the thing and Ben Jonson the man. As the audience would necessarily be select and discreet (Court influence being potent), the risk of disclosure was not serious ; and even if it had been, Jonson's skill would have been equal to the task of hoodwinking any probable audience. On this occasion luck helped cunning. In the nick of time, George Wither, a " prodigious pourer forth of rhime," happened to publish a volume of *Satirical Essays* in rhyme, with a ridiculous dedication of the thing to himself as patron and protector. This I fancy gave Jonson just what he wanted—a red herring to draw across the scent.

The *Prince's Masque* had another, and for our purpose far more significant title—*Time Vindicated to Himself and His Honours*. Time, no Time of long ago, but the age that was then passing, had been slandered, taxed with being mean and dull and sterile, and the intention of the Masque or Pageant was to refute these calumnies in presence, not of an inquisitive world, but of Time's living ornaments (as well as himself). If report speak true, it was presented on the 19th of January, 1623—the Sunday in that memorable year which fell nearest to Bacon's birthday—presented in circumstances of unprecedented splendour, " the Prince leading the Measures with the French embassador's wife." The Masque (as given in Jonson's *Works*) is sub-divided into Antimasque and Masque proper.

Fame, the accredited mouthpiece of the author, is by far the most important personage in the Antimasque. Her first business is to proclaim that she has been sent to invite to that night's " great spectacle," not the many, but the few who alone were worthy to view it. An inquisitive mob nicknamed The Curious at once begins to heckle Fame. A thrasonical personage called Chronomastix, a caricature compounded in unequal proportions of George Wither and the Ovid Junior of Jonson's *Poetaster*, then appears on the scene. Chronomastix, I may say in passing, seems to have deluded John Chamberlain, for he (J. C.) tells a correspondent that Jonson in the *Prince's Masque* " runs a risk by impersonating George Withers as a whipper of the times, which is a dangerous jest." At sight of Chronomastix The Curious jeer at Fame for not recognising their idol, while Chronomastix himself has the effrontery to call her his "mistress," and tells her it is for her sake alone that he " revells so in rime." Fame retorts (in effect) : " Away thou wretched Impostor ! My proclamation was not meant for thee or thy kind ; goe revell with thine ignorant admirers.

"TIME VINDICATED"

Let worthy names alone." Chronomastix is furious, brags of
his popularity, and appeals to The Curious to "come forth . . .
and now or never, spight of Fame, approve me." The stage
direction here runs : "At this, the Mutes come in." The first
Mute, an elephantine creature, meant of course for Jonson
himself, is about to bring forth a "male-Poem . . . that
kicks at Time already." (Jonson's Ode to Shakespeare was
probably ruminated, if not written, at the very time that this
"male-Poem" was struggling to be born.) The second Mute,
a quondam Justice—reminding one of Justice Clement in
Jonson's earliest comedy—is in the habit of carrying Chronomastix about " in his pocket " and crying "'O happy man !' to
the wrong party, meaning the *Poet*, where he meant the subject."
(This I take for a hint at the confusion of mind that must have
existed among lovers of the drama as to who Shakespeare really
was.) The succeeding pair of Mutes are, the one a printer
in disguise who conceals himself and " his presse in a hollow
tree, and workes by glow-worm light, the moon's too open " ;
the other a compositor who in " an angle inhabited by ants
will sit curled whole days and nights, and work his eyes out
for him."* The fifth Mute is a learned man, a schoolmaster,
who is turning the works of the caricature Chronomastix into
Latine. ("Some good pens "—as we learn from his letters—
were at this time engaged in turning Bacon's *Advancement
of Learning* into Latin, the " general language.") The sixth
and last Mute is a " Man of warre," reminiscent of Gullio in
the *Return from Parnassus*, who it may be remembered worships
" sweet Mr. Shakspeare," talks " nothing but Shakspeare,"
etc. Not one of the Mutes ever opens his mouth, and all that
the audience knows of them is told by The Curious, whose
function is to connect the Antimasque with the Masque and
act as nomenclators for the elephantine poet and his suite.
The Mutes came, or seemed to come, at the bidding of Chronomastix, in order to snub Fame for having insulted him. But
Chronomastix himself is the person actually snubbed by them,
seeing that they ignore him utterly. As for Fame, she treats
the Mutes very coolly, her only comment being " What a
confederacy of *Folly* is here ! "

Following hard on this observation (of Fame's) comes a
dance, in which The Curious adore Chronomastix and then
carry him off in triumph. Afterwards The Curious come up
again, and one of them, addressing Fame, asks : " Now, Fame,
how like you this ? " Another chimes in : " He scornes you,

* The words of the original are .
> " Who in an angle, where the ants inhabit,
> (The emblems of his labours) will sit curl'd," etc.   [Ed.]

and defies you, has got a *Fame* of his owne, as well as a Faction."
A third adds : " And these will deify him, to despite you."
Fame answers : " I envie not the *Apotheosis*. 'Twill prove
but deifying of a Pompion." (If The Curious had scented
what Fame was about, a retort like this would have been enough
to let them into the secret. But this hint, as well as her previous
taunt, " My hot inquisitors, what I am about is more than
you understand," was lost on them and they continue their
futile cackle.) Fame gets rid of The Curious at last by means
of the Cat and Fiddle, who, according to the stage direction,
" make sport with and drive them away."

Relieved of the presence of all who were unfit to view the
" great Spectacle" now on the point of being exhibited " with all
solemnity," Fame at last lets herself go : " Commonly (says
she) The Curious are ill-natured and, like flies, seek *Time's*
corrupted parts to blow upon, but may the sound ones live
with fame and honour, free from the molestation of these
insects."

The stage direction here runs : " Loud musique. To
which the whole scene opens, where Saturne sitting with Venus
is discovered above, and certaine Votaries coming forth below,
which are the Chorus."

Addressing the King, Fame announces that Saturn (Time)
urged by Venus (emblem of affection) had promised to set
free " certaine glories of the Time," which, though eminently
fitted to " adorn that age," had nevertheless for mysterious
reasons been kept in " darknesse" by " Hecate (Queene of
shades)." Venus puts in her word ; assures Time that the
liberation of the " glories " is a " worke (which) will prove his
honour " as well as exceed " men's hopes." Saturn answers
her gallantly and then addressing the Votaries says : " You
shall not long expect : with ease the things come forth (that)
are born to please. Looke, have you seene such lights as
these ? "

This is the very climax of the Masque. " The *Masquers*
(so runs the stage direction) are discovered and that which
obscured them vanisheth." The Votaries exclaim with rapture :
" These, these must sure some wonders be. . . . What grief,
or envie had it beene, that these and such had not beene seene,
but still obscured in shade ! Who are the glories of the *Time*
. . . and for the light were made ! "

(Who were these " glories " whom Fame, the Prince, Ben
Jonson, and the rest had with difficulty rescued from the under-
world, in whose behalf inquisitive intruders had been excluded,
about whom absurd mistakes of identity had been made, and
who according to Fame were destined to play parts in the

" apotheosis " of a pumpkin ?* The only answer that occurs to me is that the spectacle consisted essentially of a selection from among the *dramatis personæ* who were about to figure in the First Folio, especially characters out of the sixteen or twenty then unpublished plays.)

The Masque ends with an exhortation to charity, the final words being :

> Man should not hunt mankind to death,
>> But strike the enemies of man.
> Kill vices if you can :
> They are your wildest beasts :
> And when they thickest fall, you make the Gods true feasts.

(Bearing in mind that Bacon was probably regarded by the audience as an ill-used man, this exhortation sorts well with what I take to be the true interpretation of the Masque. So does the motto with which it opens. In that motto Martial bids ill-natured censors to leave him alone and keep their venom for self-admirers, persons vain of their own achievements. From first to last, therefore, *Time Vindicated* seems to have been deliberately adjusted to Bacon.)

The second part of this quasi-national scheme for doing honour to Shakespeare-Bacon falls now to be considered. The First Folio was published, it would seem, towards the end of 1623. Though not entered on the Stationers' Register till November, it may well have been on the stocks before that, for the difficulties of collecting, arranging with interested printers, editing, adapting (*The Tempest* for example), and so forth, must have been extraordinary. The volume is introduced by some doggerel, signed " B. I.," which tells the reader :

> This figure that thou here seest put,
> It was for gentle Shakespeare cut ;
> Wherein, etc.

Derision and mystification, twin motives or causes of the guy Chronomastix, are equally the motives of this grotesque " figure." Whether this were also intended to parody the doggerel inscribed on Shakespeare's gravestone in Stratford Church may be open to doubt. That inscription runs :

> Good frend, for Jesus sake forbeare
> To digge the dust encloased heare ;
> Bleste be the man, etc.

* But it was not " these ' glories '," but the Faction of Chronomastix, and the " Fame of his own," who, according to the real Fame, were destined to " deify a Pompion." The suggestion which follows that the " glories " were " a selection from among the *dramatis personæ* who were about to figure in the First Folio " is an hypothesis which will not, I fear, meet with general acceptance even among " Baconians." [ED.]

BACONIAN ESSAYS

Warned by " B. I." that laughter is in that air, we turn to the famous Ode itself which is signed " Ben : Ionson " (not " B. I.") This Poem opens with a significant hint that the " *name* " Shakespeare, as distinct from his " book " and his " *fame*," was a delicate subject to handle. After having assured himself with much ado that Shakespeare's (true) name is now in no danger, Jonson proceeds to inform him that he (Shakespeare) is alive still, " a moniment without a tombe." Then comes the line : " And though thou hadst small Latin and less Greek," which is generally mistaken for a categorical statement that Shakespeare lacked Latin, whereas it should be understood as equivalent to " Supposing thou hadst small Latin," etc. The word " would " in the next sentence (" From thence to honour thee I would not seek ") shows this to be the reading.

Then come the triumphant verses in which, after having challenged " insolent Greece or haughtie Rome " to produce a greater than Shakespeare, Jonson exclaims :

> Triumph my Britaine, thou hast one to showe,
> To whom all Scenes of Europe homage owe.
> He was not of an age, but for all time !
> And all the Muses still were in their prime,
> When like Apollo he came forth, etc.

(Compare this with what Jonson wrote of Bacon not many years later : Bacon " is he, who hath filled up all numbers ; and performed that in our tongue, which may be compared or preferred, either to insolent *Greece* or haughty *Rome*. In short, within his view and about his times were all the wits born that could honour a language, or helpe study. Now things daily fall, wits grow downe-ward, and *Eloquence* growes back-ward. So that hee may be named, and stand as the *marke* and *akme* of our language. . . . Hee seemed to mee ever, by his worke, one of the greatest men, and most worthy of admiration that had beene in many Ages." The similarity between the two eulogies strikes one the moment they are brought into juxtaposition, and this helps to explain the exclusion of the Ode from the collected *Workes of Ben : Jonson* : 1640-1.)

After this rapturous outburst the mood changes, and we are bored by a number of didactic lines about the need of toil and sweat as well as genius, " for the good poet's made as well as born." The passage is one among many symptoms of Jonson's long-standing quarrel with Shakespeareolators—a quarrel which at a later date found expression in the *Discoveries*—for refusing to see that the carelessness of their idol was at times not less conspicuous than his genius. Satisfied with having vindicated his own consistency, Jonson goes on to declare that each " well-torned and true-filed " line of Shakespeare's " seemes to shake a lance as brandished at the eyes of ignorance." (Obviously, therefore, Jonson had in view a peculiar kind of ignorance, one which the mere technique displayed in the First Folio would, but for a misunderstanding, have put to flight. The quondam Justice of *Time Vindicated* who was wont to cry " O happy man ! to the wrong party," suggests the misunderstanding in question. What, moreover, are we to make of the " stage" shaking and " lance " shaking and brandishing ? How reconcile this punning upon *shake* and *spear* with the opening lines of the Ode which breathe forth reverence for " thy name." It had been difficult, short of direct statement, to give plainer indications that Jonson was out for a juggle with a pair of names, one of them an *alias*.)

On the heels of the lance-brandishing jest comes the passionate utterance : " Sweet Swan of Avon, what a sight it were to see thee in our waters yet appeare, and make those flights upon the bankes of Thames, that so did take Eliza and our James ! " (Here *suggestio falsi* is carried to the verge of the lie. What Jonson would have us think he felt about Warwick and its Avon is one thing. What he actually thought may be gathered from a fragment of rather later date in which he jeers at " Warwick Muses " for choosing a " Hoby-horse " as their favourite mount—" the *Pegasus* that uses to waite on *Warwick* Muses," etc. Be this as it may, the ethics of the case would cause him no uneasiness. A secret had to be kept in deference to the wishes of one whom Jonson regarded as almost the greatest and most admirable of men, one too whose right to an incognito no living man of letters was likely to dispute.)

Jonson's yearning to see Shakespeare once more " upon the bankes of Thames " is suddenly arrested by a vision. Turning his poetic eye upwards and catching sight of the constellation Cygnus, he affects to be thrilled by the conceit that Shakespeare had been metamorphosed, " advanced " to a higher sphere—" the hemisphere " as he calls it. (The Ode belongs, as has been said, to 1622-23. Some ten or a dozen years earlier, Shakspere, preferring humdrum Stratford to London and poetry, had turned his back on the Capital. If this yearning had been uttered in 1612-13, instead of 1622-23, it might have been meant for the Stratford man. So with the vision and the thrill, if we could have referred them to 1616-17, they would have have provoked no question. But as things stand, question is inevitable. Had the yearning been kept under since 1612, and why ? The vision too and the thrill, what had they to do with the testator of 1616 ? What more likely than that Jonson had in his mind the social elevation of the wonderful man who long before 1623 had broken his magic wand, doffed his singing robes, and taken leave of the stage for ever ?)

The Ode closes on a note akin to despair at the low estate of Poetry ever since Shakespeare had ceased to enrich and adorn it. A similar note, it will be remembered, marks the close of Jonson's appreciation of Bacon : " Now things daily fall : wits grow downe-ward, and Eloquence growes back-ward " etc. Here again the thoughts of Jonson were evidently running on Shakespeare ; for with Jonson Eloquence was Poetry, or rather—to speak by the book—Poetry was " the most prevailing Eloquence, and of the most exalted Charact."

The contention of this article may be compressed into one sentence : The *Prince's Masque* and the famous Ode to Shakespeare were a signal act of homage in two parts to one man, and that man Francis Bacon. The proposition does not admit of demonstrative proof. High probability is all that is claimed, and if the claim be rejected the fault is with the advocate.

Such being the Preface, let us now turn to the further Essay on the Masque of *Time Vindicated*, which Edward Smithson left for, alas, posthumous publication.

Proprietas denique illa inseparabilis, quae *Tempus* ipsum sequitur, ut veritatem indies parturiat. *De Aug: Scientiarum*, 1623.

The year 1623 was a memorable one for literature. First in order of date came a masterpiece of Ben Jonson's, the Masque of *Time Vindicated*. This was followed by Bacon's *De Augmentis Scientiarum*, an expanded version of his *Advancement of Learning*, written many years earlier. The finest gift of that year was the First Folio of *Shakespeare*.

Time Vindicated consists of two violently contrasted parts ; jest and earnest, antimasque and masque proper. The most conspicuous figure in the farcical part is CHRONOMASTIX, an enigmatical creature, so greedy of publicity (for fame is denied him) that his only " end " is " to get himselfe a name," to ingratiate himself with " rumor " (he would have said *Fame*) as an inspired poet or maker.* CHRONOMASTIX is escorted by a doting mob of inquisitive adorers, the CURIOUS, who are obsessed by the expectation that they are about to assist at the deification of a great poet, their own incomparable CHRONOMASTIX as they fondly imagine. FAME, the mouthpiece of Jonson, derides the CURIOUS at every turn, and when they tell her that CHRONOMASTIX " has got a *Fame* of his owne, as well as a Faction : and these will deifie him, to despite you," FAME replies : " I envie not

---

* It might be well here to quote the original words. Chronomastix, addressing Fame, delivers himself as follows :

> " It is for you I revel so in rhyme,
> Dear Mistress, not for hope I have, the Time
> Will grow the better by it ; to serve Fame
> Is all my end, and get myself a name."

To which Fame answers :

> " Away, I know thee not, wretched impostor,
> Creature of glory, mountebank of wit,
> Self-loving braggart, Fame doth sound no trumpet
> To such vain empty fools : 'tis Infamy
> Thou serv'st, and follow'st, scorn of all the Muses !
> Go revel with thine ignorant admirers,
> Let worthy names alone."

Whereupon Chronomastix makes an appeal to his " ignorant admirers " :

> " O you, the Curious,
> Breathe you to see a passage so injurious,
> Done with despight, and carried with such tumour
> 'Gainst me, that am so much the friend of rumour ?
> I would say, Fame ?   .   .   .
> Who with the lash of my immortal pen
> Have scourg'd all sorts of vices and of men.
> Am I rewarded thus ? have I, I say,
> From Envy's self-torn praise and bays away,
> With which my glorious front, and word at large,
> Triumphs in print at my admirers' charge ?

Whereat " Ears," one of " The Curious," exclaims :

> Rare ! how he talks in verse, just as he writes !

[Ed.]

the *Apotheosis*. 'Twill prove but deifying of a Pompion." The antimasque closes with the ignominious expulsion of CHRONOMASTIX and his votaries ; obviously because the " great spectacle," which *Time* intended that " night to exhibit with all solemnity," was too august for prying eyes to see.

The Masque proper opens with an address to King James, the gist of which is that " certaine glories of the *Time*," till then artificially concealed, were about to be freed " at Love's suit " or intercession because admirably fitted " to adorne the age." The climax of the Masque follows this address almost immediately. The stage direction runs : " The *Masquers* are discovered, and that which obscur'd them, vanisheth." The CHORUS of the Masque is delighted by the vision of the *Masquers*, and cries out : " What griefe, or envie had it beene, that these, and such (as these) had not beene seene, but still obscur'd in shade ! Who are the glories of the Time, . . . and for the light were made ! "

The essential fiction of *Time Vindicated*, known also as *The Prince's Masque*, is that Time had been reproached with incapacity to produce masterpieces comparable anyway with those of Greece and Rome ; and that the revelation of these Masquers was a triumphant refutation of the calumny. To suppose that this result was achieved by the Prince and his companions would be to insult Ben Jonson, the Prince, and all concerned. The all-important feature of the revelation must have been the *make-up* of the Masquers.

For several months previous to 1623 Jonson's

mind had necessarily been concentrated on Shakespeare ; collecting manuscripts ; squaring rival publishers ; appreciating contributions offered by admirers (Fletcher perhaps and Chapman among others) ; amending originals, *Julius Cæsar* for instance ; acting as editor-in-chief of the great book ; meditating his Ode to " Shakespeare," *the man he lov'd and honoured* (*on this side idolatry*) *as much as any.* (See *Discoveries*, 1641, for this italicised passage).

There are many and various indications to justify the hypothesis that the Masque as a whole was a tribute of love and admiration for " Shakespeare." Here are some of them. (1) *Love* is the incentive to the freeing of the " wonders "—the " glories "—that so charmed the Chorus of the Masque. Love for " Shakespeare " was probably Jonson's leading motive for undertaking all the drudgery connected with the First Folio. (2) The mention of "envie" by the Chorus gives one to think. Deprecation of *envy* is the burden of the enigmatical and portentous exordium of Jonson's Ode to Shakespeare. (3) For reasons unexplained by his accredited biographers, the plays of Shakespeare had long been held back or secluded, but were then on the eve of publication or disclosure ; not indeed " cured and perfect of their limbes "—to quote the editorial figment in the First Folio—but certainly less damaged, and imperfect than even Jonson, at an earlier stage, can have expected. (4) The audience of *Time Vindicated* is given to understand that " the Bosse of *Belinsgate*," a nickname for Jonson, " has a male-*poem* in her belly now, big as a colt, that kicks at *Time* already." In my opinion this *Time*-defying *poem* was none other than the famous Ode to Shakespeare. These indications alone are sufficient to justify the above-mentioned hypothesis that the Masque as a whole was a tribute of love and admiration for " Shakespeare." On no other hypothesis would the title, *Time Vindicated*, have been appropriate or even excusable. Whereas no other conceivable title would have been so absolutely appropriate, if " Shakespeare " were, as I believe he was, the hero of the Masque ; in precisely the same sense, by the way, in which he was the hero of the Ode ; the only Poet worthy to be compared, in the words of the Ode, with " all that insolent Greece or haughtie Rome sent forth, or since did from their ashes come."

Another significant feature of the Masque is the display of anxiety to safeguard the spectacular revelation of the Masquers from the attentions of inquisitive observers, an anxiety which requires the drastic expulsion of the Curious. This anxiety, as I read it, betokened a secret intimately connected with the First Folio. Before developing this contention, it may be well to clear the ground, not only of Heminge and Condell, but also of the Stratford gentleman's representatives. Heminge and Condell were probably mere dummies who gave Jonson *carte blanche* to say in their names anything whether strictly true or not, which he thought conducive to the end in view ; the prefatory address ostensibly subscribed by them is too Jonsonian to admit of any doubt on this score. As for " Mr. Shakspere," he had long been dead and buried, and his commonplace Will knows nothing of plays, manuscripts, books, or anything that matters. And as for his representatives— had they been consulted at all—they would have welcomed, rather than vetoed publicity.

The object of these precautions to secure secrecy must have been a *persona grata* to the King, Prince, and Court; this might go without saying. A significant conjuration against hunting " Mankind to death " suggests that he was also considered, by the Prince among others, a victim of malicious persecution. For other clues we have to go back to the Antimasque. The CURIOUS have contrived to pick up several very useful items of information about the mysterious object in question. They know for instance that he is or has been served by printers and compositors so devoted to him, that they were quite content to " worke eyes out for him," in dark holes and corners, the better to " conceale " them. They know too that a typical admirer of certain " *poems*," which he was in the habit of carrying about " in his pocket," made the ridiculous mistake of addressing his congratulations " to the wrong party " : to CHRONOMASTIX, the " subject " of the Antimasque, whom he mistook for the " *Poet*." This blunder is crucial. The secret so ostentatiously safeguarded was a secret of pseudonymity. The *Poet* of the Masque (and of our quest)—the very antithesis of the blatant poetaster of the Antimasque—was a " maker " who concealed his personality behind a pen-name.

The evidence that Francis Bacon was a " concealed " poet is incontestable. A private letter of his is conclusive, though Aubrey's corroborative evidence is by no means negligible. Moreover, Bacon, besides being a *persona grata* at Court, was probably regarded by many notabilities not as a criminal, but rather as a sufferer for the faults of his day and generation. Ben Jonson's views may be gathered from his *Discoveries* (1641) where he tells that Bacon was " one of the greatest men . . . that had beene in many Ages. . . . perform'd that in our tongue which may be compar'd or preferr'd to, either insolent *Greece* or haughtie *Rome*. . . . So that hee may be nam'd and stand as the *marke* and *akme* of our language. . . . In his adversity I ever prayed that *God* would give him strength : for *Greatnesse* he could not want." Francis Bacon then was the mysterious poet of *Time Vindicated*. That Bacon was not the only concealed poet of those days is probably true. London might have teemed with concealed poets. But the only concealed poet who satisfies the many other conditions is Francis Bacon. Additional evidence that we are on the right track is supplied by the Antimasque. The " Nosed " ones among the CURIOUS have smelt out *apropos* of CHRONO-MASTIX that " a schoolmaster is turning all his workes into Latin." Now it happens that about 1623 Bacon wrote to an intimate friend : " My labours are most set to have those works . . . *Advancement of Learning* . . . the *Essays* (etc), well translated into Latin by the help of some good pens that forsake me not." The *Advancement of Learning* in Latin form, *De Aug : Scientiarum*, appeared in 1623, dedicated to Prince Charles the dedicatee of our Masque (and Camden, Jonson's "reverend" master may have helped in the translation—but this is mere conjecture).*

The figure CHRONOMASTIX is not easy to range or class ; for he is not a caricature proper. He salutes FAME with impudent assurance (in the Antimasque) as his "Deare Mistris" and tells her that "he revells so in rime" for no other "end" than "to serve *Fame* . . . and get himselfe a name." FAME, here as elsewhere, the mouthpiece of Jonson, browbeats the blatant creature : "Away, I know thee not, wretched Impostor, Creatire of glory, Mountebanke of witte, selfe-loving Braggart, . . . Scorne of all the Muses, goe revell with thine ignorant admirers, let worthy names alone." A little abashed by this rebuff, CHRONOMASTIX appeals to the CURIOUS for sympathy ; tells them that his "glorious front and word at large triumphs in print at my admirers charge" ; and finishes his harangue by this invitation to his friends and admirers : "Come forth that love me, and now or never, spight of *Fame*, approve me." CHRONOMASTIX therefore whatever he be, is the very antithesis of a self-effacing poet or maker. He belongs I think to the

---

* In Mr. Smithson's *Shakespeare-Bacon*, at p. 124, we read : "A schoolmaster, for example, is engaged in turning 'all his (Chronomastix's) workes' from the insular 'English in which they were originally written into the general or continental Latine.'" It is somewhat difficult however, to find Bacon under the guise of Chronomastix.

Jonson's words are : ·

> "There is a school-master
> Is turning all his works too into Latin,
> To pure Satyric Latin ; makes his boys
> To learn him ; call's him the Times Juvenal ;
> Hangs all his school with his sharp sentences ;
> And o'er the execution place hath painted
> Time whipt, for terror to the infantry."

This also appears to be an allusion to George Wither. [ED.]

same genus as those fantastic portraits, *Landru chez lui*, etc., lately exhibited in Piccadilly by the National Portrait Society, partly to amuse the public and partly to puzzle quidnuncs. He was a freak in other words, and his function was to amuse outsiders and put curiosity off the scent.

Turn we now from the figure CHRONOMASTIX, to the " Figure " which mars the front page of the First Folio : the sorry " Figure . . . wherein the Graver had a strife with Nature to out-doo the life " ; as " B. J." (Ben Jonson) significantly informs " the Reader." " B. J.'s " innuendo does not stop here ; he follows it up by explicitly warning all readers to " looke not on " the " picture," but on the " Booke." The warning seems almost superfluous ; for the effigy cannot be identified with portrait or bust of any human being. Twin brother to CHRONOMASTIX, the thing is a freak expressly designed to prevent inquisitive persons, ourselves among others, from scrutinising the fiction then launched on the world.

Reverting once more to the Antimasque and the orgiastic dance at the end of which the CURIOUS carry away their deity CHRONOMASTIX : one or other of the deluded adorers taunts FAME in these words : " He scornes you and defies you, h'as got a *Fame* on's owne, as well as a Faction, and these will deifie him, to despite you." FAME replies : " I envie not the *Apotheosis*. 'Twill prove but deifying of a Pompion." When these words were spoken, it is quite possible that neither the figure, nor the Ode, nor the prefatory addresses had reached finality. But Jonson's inside knowledge of the whole project would enable him to forecast important results. One of these results, in my opinion, was that a Pumpkin would be deified by posterity. In this forecast a note of misgiving is perceptible enough ; but of spitefulness there is hardly a trace ; for after all, the pumpkin is a *deserving* vegetable—the stress here is on the word *deserving*, since that is the epithet by which the surviving Burbages, in perfect good temper, described the deceased Shakspere. This apotheosis idea, I may add, is also prominent in the Shakespeare Ode at the point where Jonson pulls himself up : " But stay, I see thee to the hemisphere advanced and made a constellation there." In the Ode however the apostrophe—half banter, half congratulation—is entirely free from regret or misgiving.

From the point of view of the privileged few who were in the secret, *Time Vindicated* and the Shakespeare Folio were, I consider, parts of a superlative Act of Homage to the greatest of modern poets. From Jonson's special point of view they were a pious fraud, in which at the behest of disinterested love and admiration for Bacon, he consented to undertake the chief rôle. After the death of Bacon Jonson's mood may have undergone some modification. Certain it is that the Ode, his finest poem, is excluded from the first edition, Vol. II, of his collected Works, and that in his *Discoveries* he tells " posterity " certain truths about Shakespeare which were not even suggested in the Ode.

Hitherto our thoughts have been preoccupied with Ben Jonson. They shall now be devoted more closely to Bacon and the state of his mind and feelings about 1623. In a pathetic letter of his to King James, Bacon comforts himself with the knowledge that his fall was not the " act " of his Sovereign, and then proceeds : " For now it is thus with me : I am a year and a half old in misery . . . mine own means through mine own improvidence are poor and weak. . . . My dignities remain marks of your favour, but burdens of my present fortune. The poor remnants . . . of my former fortunes in plate and jewels I have spread upon poor men unto whom I owed, scarcely leaving myself bread. . . . I have often been told by many of my Lords (of your Council), as it were in excusing the severity of the sentence, that they knew they left me in good hands. . . . Help me, dear Sovereign . . . so far as I . . . that desire to live to study, may not be driven to study to live."

Here it is to be observed that the proceeds of sale of the Shakespeare Folio, " printed at his admirers charge," would help towards relieving the fallen man's pecuniary distress, whilst the august compliment conveyed by the Masque would tend to soothe his lacerated feelings.

The attitude of a concealed poet to his art is rarely explicit, or concealment would be next to impossible. In this connection I ask leave to quote from an Essay, *Shakespeare-Bacon*, by E. W. S., published many years ago.* The essayist, after having stated that Bacon's qualifications for dramatic work were of a high order, and that some at least of his recognised Elizabethan

* Swan Sonnenschein & Co., 1899.

output actually were dramatic, runs on : " More-over, curious as is Bacon's manner when treating of ' poesie,' his manner when dealing with dramatic poetry is more curious still. The *Advancement of Learning* though not published till the reign of her successor, belongs to the age of Queen Elizabeth, in conception, observation, reflection, and substance generally. In this work, after having mapped out the " globe " of human knowledge into three great continents of which poetry is one, he finds himself face to face with dramatic poetry. Compelled to give the thing a name, he rejects the almost inevitable word *dramatic*, in favour of the distant word *repre-sentative*. And what he permits himself to say about ' representative ' poetry, in that the natural, and appropriate place for saying it, seems intended to suggest—what of course was absurdly untrue—that he was all but a stranger to anything in the nature of a dramatic performance. The suggestion too is strangely out of keeping with passages of unexpected occurrence in other parts of the book. For instance, in handling what he calls the ' Georgics of the mind,' he describes poetry (along with history) in terms which so admirably characterise the very best dramatic poetry of the age, that it is difficult to resist the conviction that he must have been thinking chiefly of the masterpieces of Shakespeare. 'In poetry,' says he, 'we may find painted forth with great life, how affections are kindled and incited ; and how pacified and refrained ; and how again contained from act and further degree ; how they disclose themselves, how they work, how they vary, how they gather and fortify, how they are inwrapped one with another, and how they do fight and encounter one with another . . . how to set affection against affection, and to master one by another ; even as we use to hunt beast with beast,' etc. Another of these unexpected passages seems to imply that Bacon, writing at the close of the Elizabethan epoch, was so convinced of the paramount importance of dramatic poetry, as to have forgotten that there was any poetry at all, except what had to do with the theatre. In this passage Bacon has been claiming that 'for expressing the affections, passions, corruptions, and customs, we are more beholding to the poets than to the philosophers '—at this point he suddenly breaks off with an ironical : ' But it is not good to stay too long in the theatre.'*

A question that has probably been intriguing some of my readers is : Why did Bacon abandon the poet's Crown to which his genius entitled him ? From among the complex of conceivable reasons it will suffice to pick out three. (1) In dedicating the *De Augmentis Scientiarum* to Prince Charles, 1623, Bacon writes : " It is a book I think will live, and be a citizen of the world which English books are not." Again, a letter, of about the same date, to an intimate friend contains this passage : " For these modern languages will play the bankrowtes with books ; and since I have lost much time with this age, I would be glad, as God shall give me leave, to recover it with posterity." " *Play the bank-rowtes* " means, I suppose, put a stop to the currency ; and " *lost much time with this age* "

* *Shakespeare-Bacon* pp. 89-91, and Note 2 on p. 91.

is probably an allusion to pseudonymous work. These and similar passages justify the conclusion that by this time Bacon had convinced himself that English as a literary language, was doomed to go under to Latin. (2) The poet in Bacon, as in Wordsworth and others, had expired with the passing of youth. (3) Bacon imagined himself the Discoverer of a New Instrument or method, by which human life would be so beatified that posterity would revere him as one of its greatest benefactors ; *if* only men of science (such as Harvey) were for ever deprived of excuse for pooh-poohing the *Novum Organum*, merely because its inventor was none other than Shakespeare, sonneteer and dreamer of dreams.

[*Note by the Editor*]. There appears to be no doubt that in " Chronomastix " Jonson was lampooning George Wither, whose " Abuses Stript and Whipt, or Satiricall Essayes," was published by Budge in 1622, (there had been an earlier edition in 1613) and was followed by a poem called "The Scourge." In " Abuses Stript and Whipt " we find the following lines :

> And though full loth, 'cause their ill natures urge,
> I'll send abroad a satire with a scourge,
> That to their shame for this abuse shall strip them,
> And being naked in their vices whip them.
> And to be sure of those that are most rash
> Not one shall 'scape him that deserves the lash.

There is also an Epigram to " Time," in which Wither asks :

> Now swift-devouring, bald, and ill-fac't Time,
> Dost not thou blush to see thyself uncloak't ?

Another Epigram is to " Satyro-Mastix," the last lines of which are :

> Then scourge of Satyrs hold thy whip from mine,
> Or I will make my rod lash thee and thine.

" Wither's Motto " (1621) was " *nec habeo nec careo nec curo.*"   This was satirised by John Taylor, the Water-Poet, in the words " et habeo, et careo, et curo," and is obviously alluded to in Jonson's Masque, where " *Nose* " says " The gentleman-like *Satyre* cares for nobody."

Wither, moreover, quarrelled with the Stationers' Company and the printers (who disapproved of his independent method of business), which also was a subject for Jonson's ridicule in the Masque :

> One is his Printer in disguise, and keepes
> His presse in a hollow tree, where to conceale him,
> He workes by glow-worme light, the moon's too open,
>   etc., etc.

In the *Dict : of National Biography* we are told that " Jonson quarrelled with Alex. Gill the elder for having quoted Wither's work with approval in his ' Logonomia Anglica ' (1619), and Jonson revenged himself by caricaturing Wither under the title of ' Chronomastix ' in the Masque of *Time Vindicated* presented at Court 1623-4," and allusion is made to Jonson's sarcasm with regard to Wither's quarrel with his printers.

Further, we find John Chamberlain writing to Sir Dudley Carleton, on January 25, 1622-3, as follows with reference to the Masque of *Time Vindicated* : " Ben Jonson they say is like to hear of it on both sides of the head for personating

"TIME VINDICATED"

George Withers, a poet or poetaster he terms him, as hunting after some, by being a Chronomastix, or whipper of the time, which is become so tender an argument that it must not be admitted either in jest or earnest." (*The Court and Times of James the First*. Ed. 1848. Vol. II, p. 356.)

These facts seem to have been well known to Mr. Smithson, for not only does he quote John Chamberlain's letter in his *Nineteenth Century* article, where he expresses the opinion that " Chronomastix " is " a caricature compounded in unequal proportions of George Wither and the Ovid Junior of Jonson's *Poetaster* (as to which see an interesting chapter in *Shakespeare-Bacon*, headed " A Caricature of some Notable Elizabethan Poet," together with the chapter following), but among his manuscripts were found certain Notes with reference to George Wither which I cite lower down. It will be seen, however, that he was convinced that Jonson, while lampooning and ridiculing Wither, the scourger of the time, had for his main object the glorification of the Shakespearean drama under cover of a *Masque*—those glorious works wherein " Time," which had been vilified by Wither, found its all-sufficient and splendid " Vindication."*

---

* It may perhaps be worth while to quote some of the words put into the mouth of " Fame " when " the whole Scene opens," and Saturn sitting with Venus is discovered above, and certain " Votaries " come forth below, " which are the chorus," shortly before " the Masquers are discovered."

> " Within yond' darkness, Venus hath found out
> That Hecate, as she is queen of shades,
> Keeps certain glories of the time obscured,
> There for herself alone to gaze upon
> As she did once the fair Endymion.
> These Time hath promised at Love's suit to free

BACONIAN ESSAYS

The following are Mr. Smithson's Notes to which I have made reference :
" Wither sends

> Abroad a Satyr with a scourge ;
> That to their shame for this abuse shall strip them,
> And being naked in their vices whip them.
>> (*Abuses Stript and Whipt.* Ed. 1622, p. 305.)

He gives Justices of Peace a warning lest they be put out of the Commission for partiality (p. 318). Ruffling Cavaliars also are touched (p. 320).

In the address to the reader of *Shepheard's Hunting*, Wither to some extent recants his disgust at Time—says he has been ' persuaded to entertain a better opinion of the Times than I lately conceived, and assured myself, that Virtue had far more followers than I supposed.' Curiously enough, therefore, Wither's frame of mind in 1622* seems to have been similar to that of Jonson in *Time Vindicated*. The coincidence would help perhaps to mislead the judgment of the time, and may have so commended itself to Jonson.

> As being fitter to adorn the age.
> By you [i.e., King James] restored on earth, most like his own ;
> And fill this world of beauty here, your Court."

What were the " certain glories of the time obscured " which Time had " promised at Love's suit to free " is matter for speculation.

* But *Shepheard's Hunting* appeared in 1615. Jonson, in the Grand Chorus at the end of the Masque, writes :—

> " Turn hunters then
> Again
>> But not of men.
> Follow his ample
>> And just example,
> That hates all chase of malice, and of blood,
>> And studies only ways of good.
> To keep soft peace in breath
>> Man should not hunt mankind to death,
> But strike the enemies of man.
>> Kill vices if you can," etc.

Here was yet another hit at George Wither, but who was he whose " ample and just example " was held up as a model for imitation ? [ED.]

I don't think Wither knows why, or by whom he was persecuted. (See Philarate to Willy in Eclogue I, and last page but two of 'Address to the Reader.')

He calls Time 'bald and ill-fac'd,' 'shameless time,' speaks of his 'deformities,' 'blockish age,' that 'truth' in this age gets 'hatred,' 'while love and charitie are fled to heaven.'

He took upon him to scourge Time, and he was certainly arrogant enough, in form at any rate, for Chronomastix.

I therefore take him to have been the stalking-horse or blind used by Jonson, the Prince, and some others, to conceal the true object."

SHAKESPEARE—A THEORY

SHAKESPEARE—A THEORY

*[The Notes of this Essay (except those inserted by the
Editor) which are denoted by Roman Numerals, will
be found at the end of it.]*

THE recent discovery of an entry in a domestic
expenses account book of the Mannours or Manners
family has attracted some notice. According to
Mr. Sidney Lee* the terms of the entry, under the
head "Payments for household stuff, plate,
armour," etc., are: "1613. Item 31 Martii
to Mr. Shakspeare in gold about my Lorde's
impreso [the terminal *o* should be *a*] xliiij$^{s.}$, to
Richard Burbadge for paynting and making yt in
gold xliiij$^{s.}$. [Total] iiij^{li}viij^{s}." An impresa Camden describes as "a device in picture with his motto
or word borne by noble and learned personages to
notifie some particular conceit of their own," its
nearest modern analogue being the book-plate.†

---

* Mr. Smithson's references to Sir Sidney as Mr. Lee show that
this Essay was written many years ago. [Ed.]

† But an *impresa* was much more than this. *Imprese* were employed
in tournaments (e. g.). Puttenham says, "The Greeks call it Emblema,
the Italians Impresa, and we a Device, such as a man may put into
letters of gold and send to his mistresses for a token, or cause to be em-
broidered in Scutcheons of arms on any bordure of a rich garment, to
give by his novelty marvel to the beholder." On this matter of the
Earl of Rutland's *Impresa* (it was Francis Manners, the Sixth Earl for
whom the work was executed), see my "*Is there a Shakespeare Problem?*"
pp. 16-21. It is to be noted that in the year 1613, after all the great
Shakespearean works had been written, we find Shakspere, the (alleged)
great dramatist, then, as we must assume, at the zenith of his fame,
engaged with his fellow-actor, Dick Burbage, to work at Lord Rutland's
new Device, for the magnificent reward of 44^{s}. ! [Ed.]

Burbage seems to have made, as well as painted, the thing. What there was for Mr. Shakespeare to do is by no means clear. The motto, if motto there were, would to a certainty be designated by the " noble and learned personage " himself. Moreover, some three years later (1616) Burbage appears to have executed a similar commission for the same Earl of Rutland, entirely without assistance. That the clerk who made the entry denied to Burbage the " prefix of gentility " which he bestowed upon " Mr. Shakespeare " is a fact of trivial import. If —to take an imaginary case—Nick Bottom had been living " on his means " at South Place, Stratford-at-the-Bow, this clerk would have dubbed him Mr. Bottom as a matter of course in the same circumstances. Mr. Lee is of opinion that " the recovered document discloses a capricious sign of homage on the part of a wealthy and cultured nobleman to Shakespeare." If he had suggested that the two-guinea payment to " Mr. Shakespeare " may have been preceded by a hearty meal in the buttery, without exciting any feeling of resentment on the part of either recipient that the meal was not served in the dining-hall, I should have been more disposed to agree with him.

The situation is a curious one. But any serious discussion of it would be premature until we are actually in possession of the " rich harvest of new disclosures " which Mr. Lee teaches us to expect.*   Meanwhile the Bacon theory regarded as a development of the hypothesis that Shakespeare was a pen-name of Bacon's is certainly not

* Alas, that rich harvest has never seen the light. [Ed.]

crushed, if it be not actually encouraged, by this Belvoir disclosure, since no one in his senses would think of denying the existence of " Mr. Shakespeare " or his acquaintance with Richard Burbage.

In Gilbert Wats' English version (1640) of Bacon's *Instauratio Magna*, Francis Bacon, Baron of Verulam, Vicont St. Alban, who is designated as " Tertius a Platone Philosophiæ Princeps," is represented pen in hand, tall hat on head, a voluminous lace ruff round his neck, in the act of inditing : *Mundus Mens Connubio Jungam Stabili.** On the opposite page two worlds, a *Mundus Visibilis* and a *Mundus Intellectualis* are shown clasping hands across space, in order, no doubt, to give emphasis to the idea of a world and mind *connubium*. The picture typifies the conception of Bacon which has prevailed ever since. A skater on his way to the Engadine declared he was at a loss to understand why anyone ever went to Switzerland in summer for *pleasure*. Some of us would have been tempted to smile at the remark. But the prevailing conception of Bacon is probably quite as inadequate as this skater's conception of Switzerland. The age of Queen Elizabeth probably had no presage—not a hint—that Francis Bacon would ever develop into a " prince of philosophy." In my opinion the Bacon known to it was not a natural philosopher[1] even in aspiration, but an artist —an artist in words, who, if circumstances, more especially family circumstances, had been favourable

* In the portrait Bacon has an open book before him, across whose pages are written the words " *Instaur* " and " *Magna*." On the left-hand page appear the words " *Mundus Mens*," and on the right-hand page the words " *connubio jungam stabili*." [Ed.]

any time between 1580 and 1590 would have openly confessed that poetry was his ideal, and declared himself a poet. As it was, he took the line of least friction, and sooner or later acquired the title of " concealed poet." How far the concealment extended in the early days it is impossible to discover. To Sir Philip Sidney,[2] Sir J. Harrington, and other accomplished young men of their class, the true state of the case was doubtless an open secret.

Professor Nichol (*Francis Bacon*, Part I), though he thinks that Bacon " did not write Shakespeare's plays," considers that " there is something startling in the like magnificence of speech in which they find voice for sentiments, often as nearly identical when they anticipate as when they contravene the manners of thought and standards of action that prevail in our country in our age. They are similar in this respect for rank," etc. Shelley discerned that Bacon " was a poet," and Macaulay perceived that the " poetical faculty " was " powerful " in Bacon. Taine held that Bacon " thought as artists and poets habitually think," that he was one of the finest of a " poetic line," that " his mental *procédé* was that of the creator, not reasoning but intuition." Bacon, then, was essentially a poet, belonged to the same race as Sidney for example. Sidney died young, and his poetic activity ceased some time before he died. Yet Sidney's poetical achievement has come down to our day. What has become of Bacon's poetical achievement ? Was it also concealed ?

Hallam, in the *Introduction to the Literature of*

Europe, confessed he was unable to identify " the young man who came up from Stratford, was afterwards an indifferent player in a London theatre, and retired to his native place in middle life, with the author of Macbeth and Lear." Emerson (*Representative Men*) declared : " The Egyptian verdict of Shakespearean societies comes to mind, that Shakespeare[3] was a jovial actor and manager. I cannot marry this fact to his verse. Other admirable men have led lives in some sort of keeping with their thought ; but this man in wide contrast." It would be easy to adduce other evidence pointing in the same direction. But Hallam and Emerson, unexceptionable witnesses, will serve the turn. On one side, then, we are brought into contact with a poet or maker whose poems elude us. On another side we are confronted with poems whose poet or maker eludes us—some of us. What if Shakespeare were to Bacon what Callisthenes, Aristophanes' actor-friend, was to Aristophanes ? Suppose by way of working hypothesis that such was the case, that Shakespeare was a pen-name of Bacon's. In that case his ultimate intention as to dropping or retaining the mask of pseudonymity would be affected by various considerations extending far beyond the family circle. (a) To be " rewarded of " the stage-manager was probably nothing less than degrading to a man of good birth. (b) The conditions under which the hypothetical Shakespeare must have written, were unfavourable to careful work. A man who is half ashamed of what he is doing is hardly likely to do his best, especially when more or less concealed. Certainly many of the plays suffer from faulty construction, inconsistency, obscurity, bombast and so forth, and what is more important, Shakespeare himself[4] was probably quite as conscious of these blemishes as were any of his critics. (c) With us the daily paper exerts a certain influence on public opinion. In Bacon's day the theatre was one of the most effective means of appeal to any considerable audience, and in that way the name Shakespeare probably got entangled in controversies with which Bacon felt no desire to meddle autonymously.[5] (d) The moral tendency of Shakespearean work published before 1609, *Venus and Adonis* for example, was not such as to forward any of the hypothetical author's schemes for place. (e) Early in the seventeenth century Bacon seems to have convinced himself that for purposes of moment Latin was destined to supplant English. He was haunted moreover by fear of impending civil commotions, and augured ill for that " fair weather learning which needs the nursing of luxurious leisure." (f) Had there been no other considerations than these, Bacon, even after he became Solicitor-General, might have been induced himself to give to the world some at least of his hypothetical offspring really " perfect of their limbes as he conceived them." It is not to be supposed that he would ever have claimed all or nearly all that passed for Shakespeare's. Much would have been disavowed altogether, and many of the more inconvenient things would, quite fairly, have been ascribed to collaboration, misprints, inexperience, haste, carelessness, etc. But the action of the ill-conditioned group which in 1609 engineered the publication of the *Sonnets* of Shakespeare, must have greatly reduced the chance that Bacon would ever consent to edit anything of Shakespeare's. So far as intimate friends were concerned, the piratical publication, however irritating,[6] would be comparatively innocuous, and as for charitable strangers, they might be trusted to discover extenuating circumstances in the youth of the author and the fashion of the time. But the great indiscriminating public, unaccustomed to make allowances, and led by an enemy like Sir Edward Coke, would chortle over the self-revelations suggested by the book, and put the worst construction on everything. Rather than face such a prospect, Bacon would be willing to pay almost any price, and the price he may be supposed to have paid was to seem to know nothing and care nothing about " Shakespeare " or anything that was his. Adherence to this policy would not necessarily involve any visible change of attitude or conduct. On the contrary, the hypothetical Shakespeare would be urged to hold on his usual course by the fear that any sudden stoppage, of the supply of plays for instance, might arouse suspicions which otherwise would have slept. Parenthetically it may be observed that Bacon had already known what it was to give to the world things—the Essays of 1597—which he would rather have kept back, but was compelled to publish because " to labour the state of them had been troublesome and subject to interpretation."

The parting between Prospero and Ariel has

been thought to adumbrate the farewell of Shakespeare, whoever he was, to Poetry—a view that is plausible enough. It would explain the position assigned to *The Tempest* in the First Folio, and suggest an interesting answer to the question why Prospero, who " prized his books above his dukedom " threatened—only threatened—to drown a particular " book." But no one knows within several years when *The Tempest* was written. Nor is it at all certain that the poem was wholly Shakespeare's.* For anything we know to the contrary, the editor of the First Folio may have interpolated the striking invocation—to mention one passage only—which begins : " Ye elves of hills."[7] *The Tempest* then, does not enable us to fix the date of Shakespeare's practical renunciation of poetry. I say, *practical* renunciation, because certain passages in *Henry the Eighth* which feelingly represent the insecurity of greatness might *ex hypothesi* have been contributed by Bacon just after his fall, though his practical renunciation could hardly have taken place later than 1612.† But whether the date were 1612 or somewhat earlier, the hypothetical Shakespeare was amply provided with other interests and

---

* I venture to refer to my short article on *The Tempest* in " The New World " of April, 1921. The reader may also profitably consult Mr. Looney's " *Shakespeare* " *Identified* on this matter, at p. 513. [Ed.]

† The better opinion now seems to be that *Henry VIII* is not Shakespearean, but was written by Fletcher and Massinger in collaboration. Mr. James Spedding long ago tendered reasons which have convinced most of the " orthodox " critics that the better part of this play, including Wolsey's and Buckingham's speeches, was the work of Fletcher, and recently Mr. Dugdale Sykes, in his *Sidelights on Shakespeare*, published at the " Shakespeare Head Press " at Stratford-upon-Avon (1919), with preface by the late A. H. Bullen, appears to have proved that all that part of this great spectacular drama which was not written by Fletcher came from the pen of Massinger, who, as we know, frequently collaborated with him. [Ed.]

pursuits. (a) Rhetoric had long held a high place in his affections. " Rhetoric and Logic," says he, " these two, rightly taken, are the gravest of the sciences, being the arts of arts,"[8] and what excellence he attained in the former of these arts we know from Ben Jonson. (b) Though poesy, the recreation of his leisure—Bacon would never have allowed that it was anything but a recreation—were denied him, prose, splendid inimitable prose was his to command. (c) The delightful days and months and years which he had spent with poets both ancient and modern, particularly Ovid,[9] might be turned to philosophical account. (d) Historical projects allured him. In the *Advancement of Learning*, a history—a prose history no doubt—of England from the " Wars of the Roses " downwards is noted as a desideratum, and seems to have been begun. The *History of the Reign of King Henry VII* (1622), however, is the only portion of the desiderated history which reached completeness. (e) Legislative projects also attracted him, less strongly no doubt than historical. (f) But at this time the *Great Instauration* had possessed itself of the chief place in his affection : " Of this I can assure you that though many things of great hope decay with youth,[10] yet the proceeding in that work doth gain upon me, upon affection and desire," he writes, about 1609, to his bosom friend Matthew. The instauration, say rather transfiguration, of human knowledge—that was the vision which now fascinated him. When the spell began to work it is difficult to determine. Early in the seventeenth century his conception of human

" learning " or " knowledge " or " science "—three words to which he attached practically the same meaning—included Poetry, not as an appendix, but as one of three fundamental constituents. Perhaps the word " culture," with " barbarism " for antithesis, would now come nearest to what he then meant by learning. The *Advancement of Learning* is the work not of a scholar in the technical sense, but of an omnivorous apprehensive imaginative reader. It is the expression by an artist in words of the serried thoughts of a mind steeped in poetry, deep versed in human nature, but certainly not versed in natural philosophy as understood by his contemporaries—Galileo for example, Gilbert and others. A passage in the first of its two books runs : " No man that wadeth in learning or contemplation thoroughly but will find printed in his heart *nil novi super terram*." It is incredible that Bacon can at this time have caught so much as a glimpse of the " New Logic," " New Art," or—to give its latest name—*Novum Organum*, which he afterwards declared was " quite new. totally new in every kind.[11] But though the *Advancement* was in fact a plea for culture, in Bacon's intention it was a serious attempt to grapple with philosophy, an attempt so serious that he afterwards declared the *Novum Organum* itself to be the " same argument sunk deeper." Moreover, in my opinion, it was his first serious attempt in that direction, hence its importance to any right apprehension of his genius.[12]

About the year 1609, the philosophical enthusiasm reached a climax. *Cogitata et Visa de*

Interpretatione Naturæ, Redargutio Philosophiarum, Sapientia Veterum, and other pieces, some of which Boswell, one of his executors, seems to have called *impetus philosophici*, were thrown off in rapid succession. As early as 1610, however, he solicits the King to employ him in writing a history of his Majesty's "Time," a hint surely that the philosophical impetus had begun to abate. The change, whether it began that year, or a year or two later, is intelligible enough. Science had not claimed him her deliverer. Harvey is reported to have sneered at his philosophy. Gilbert and Napier may have started the sneer ; for Bacon obviously under-valued mathematics, and spoke almost contemptuously of Gilbert (whom Galileo fully appreciated). About this time, too, he probably began to suspect that somewhere in the *New Art*, there lurked a defect which would have to be cured before the apparatus would work. The truth is that in the philosophical work published or privately circulated by Bacon before 1610, though there was much to appeal to the æsthetic side of the human mind, much to stimulate the cultivated layman's admiration for knowledge, for the devoted student of science there was very little help of a constructive kind, the only kind of help he really needed.[13]

The *Sapientia Veterum,* 1609, is based on a number of myths selected from the poets and fabulists of antiquity in virtue of a certain congruity with Bacon's intuitions and predilections. *The Sylva Sylvarum or Natural History*, his latest work, is based on an assemblage of what by way of distinction might be called facts. The dissonance between the two works is amazing. The *Sapientia*, which was intended to bespeak a favourable hearing for the New Art, busies itself with venerable fictions. From the *Natural History* on the other hand, poetry and fable were to have been rigorously excluded. Bacon's biographer, Rawley, wrote for the first edition of the work (1627), an address " To the Reader," which winds up : " I will conclude with an usual speech of his lordship's ; that this work of his Natural History is the world as God made it, and not as man made it ; for it hath nothing of imagination."

Several years before the *Sylva* was written, Galileo had censured as paper philosophers certain contemporaries of his, who set about the investigation of nature as if she were a " book like the Æneid or the Odyssey." One at least of Bacon's intimate friends, Sir Tobie Mathew, was no stranger to Padua and Florence, and it is quite possible that he may have informed Bacon of these strictures of Galileo's not long after they were uttered. But, be this as it may, a momentous change must have taken place after 1609, not in Bacon's aspiration to be the greatest of human benefactors to man, but in his conception of the means by which his vast expectations were to be realised. Had the change been less than " fundamental," " a good and well ordered Natural History " would not have been described in the *Phenomena Universi* (1622), as holding the " keys both of sciences and of operations." After 1612 Bacon became for some eight or nine years so immersed in affairs, as Attorney-General, Privy Councillor—no sinecure then—

Lord Chancellor, etc., that it must have been impossible for him to give to his New Logic a tithe of the attention it required. " At this period," says Dr. Abbott : " there is a great gap in the series of Bacon's philosophical works. In 1613 he was appointed Attorney-General, and from that time till 1620 no literary work of any kind published or unpublished is known to have issued from his pen. All that he did was apparently to rewrite repeatedly and revise the *Novum Organum*.[14] The *Organum* made its appearance in 1620 with a dedication to the King by no means confident of either the worth or the use of his offering. But as he says in the *proemium* that " all other ambition whatsoever was in his opinion lower than the work in hand," one would infer that his zeal for philosophy had begun to revive even before the tragedy of 1621. The remaining five years of the great man's life—" a long cleansing week of five years' expiation and more," he calls it—were more or less distracted with anxieties in no way connected with philosophy. He hoped, nevertheless, to present the old King with a " good history of England, and a better digest " of the laws, and the young King with a history of the " time and reign of King Henry the Eighth."[15] But after the most distressful *sequelæ* of his fall had been relieved, his grandiose, imposing scheme for the renovation or transfiguration of philosophy must have regained the position it had held some ten or a dozen years earlier. Without it, life for him would have been a mean and melancholy failure. " God hath framed the mind of man as a mirror or glass capable of the image of the universal world, and joyful to receive the impression thereof . . . and not delighted in beholding the variety of things and vicissitude of times, but raised also to find out the ordinances which throughout all those changes are infallibly observed."[16] This capacity, this wonder-working exaltation of the mind had been neglected, and all but lost, by reason of the interference of Aristotle and other insolent dictators, and Bacon imagined himself destined to rehabilitate it, to usher in a new era, to endow the human race, not with knowledge alone, but with legions of beneficent arts,[17] and for reward to go down to the ages as preeminently the Friend of man.[18] Compared with a vision so magnificent, his youthful dream of a poet's immortality would seem paltry, stale, and unprofitable. No wonder the old love, poetry, was forsaken. The wonder would have been if for the sake of the old love he had done or permitted or countenanced anything which he thought might possibly prejudice posterity against the new love, his " darling philosophy."[19]

The more vulnerable points of this tentative theory[20] of Bacon's relation to poetry seem to be three. First, Bacon's final perseverence in ignoring his hypothetical offspring. Second, his *Translation of certain Psalms into English Verse* which, according to Dr. Abbott, " so clearly betrays the cramping influence of rhyme and verse, that it could hardly have been the work of a true poet even of a low order." Third, the detailed treatment of poetry in the *Advancement of Learning* is essentially and flagrantly defective. Objection number one—

Bacon's persistent neglect of the plays—is easily answered.[21] The reasons for continuing to ignore them may in the aggregate have been even more cogent at the close, than at the opening of his career. For a Lord Chancellor, one who had been a " principal councillor and instrument of monarchy," to publish not verses merely, but common plays, would have been a disgrace to the peerage, and ingratitude, if not disloyalty, to the sovereign to whom he owed his many promotions. Amongst the reasons for concealment, which did not exist at the opening of life, two more may be mentioned : one, the publication of the *Sonnets*, has been sufficiently discussed ; the other, solicitude for the *Great Instauration*, has not. In casting about for an explanation of his frigid reception by contemporary science, Bacon must have hit upon a suspicion, shared maybe by King James,[22] that his true greatness after all lay rather in the domain of poetry than in that of philosophy.[23] Disappointed in his contemporaries, he would turn to the ages unborn, resolved that they at any rate should not start with a bias against his message. Any suggestion therefore, that he should allow his true name to be put to a volume of poetry, so distinguished from versified theology, would be unconditionally rejected.

To the objection founded on the *Translation of certain Psalms into English Verse* several answers suggest themselves. No artist is always at his best, least of all in illness and old age, and the *Translation* belongs to 1624 when Bacon was recovering from an attack of a painful disease. In the delightful preface to his select edition of Wordsworth's Poems, Matthew Arnold writes: " Work altogether inferior, work quite uninspired, flat and dull, is produced by him (Wordsworth) with evident unconsciousness of its defects and he presents it to us with the same faith and seriousness as his best work." Yet no competent judge of poetry would think of denying that Wordsworth was a " true poet " of a " high order."* Again, conventional feeling may have been partly responsible for the dullness of this *Translation*. Dr. Abbott surely underrates the consequence of his admission that " theological verse like theological sculpture might seem to require something of the archaic, and a close adherence to the simplicity of the original prose." Grant that Bacon was under the influence of some such feeling, and the objection we are considering is virtually answered, such was " Bacon's versatility in adapting language to the slightest shade of circumstance and purpose." Once more, the evidence that Bacon was a " concealed poet " is strong enough to hold its own against every argument that can fairly be urged against it, and to concealment dissimulation is apt to prove indispensable. It was so considered by Bacon, and Bacon's experience of the device was extensive, if not unique. In a famous Essay he carefully distinguishes between Simulation and Dissimulation, and lets it be seen that he regarded the former as

---

* Milton's versification of the Psalms is much worse than Bacon's, and if there were any doubt as to the authorship of *Paradise Lost*, and *Lycidas*, and *L'Allegro*, and *Il Penseroso*, and Milton were known only as the writer of this versification of the Psalms, it would be confidently asserted that he could not possibly be the author of the above-mentioned works. [ED.]

positively culpable, the latter as not only per-
missible but necessary.[24] A man dissimulates
when he " lets fall signs or arguments that he is
not that he is. . . . He that will be secret must
be a dissembler in some degree. For men are too
cunning to suffer a man to keep an indifferent
carriage. . . . They will so beset a man with
questions and draw him on and pick it out of him,
that without an absurd silence he must show
inclination one way. . . . So that no man can be
secret except he give himself a little scope of
dissimulation ; which is as it were but the skirts
or train of secrecy." The application is obvious.
Bacon's *Translation of Certain Psalms* is uninspired,
lacks " choiceness of phrase . . . the sweet
falling of the clauses," etc ! Why ? Possibly
because the author " is letting fall signs or arguments that he is not that he is ! " The fact that
a thing so trivial as this *Translation* should have
been published, instead of being reserved for private
circulation only—published too on the heels of the
Shakespeare First Folio—lends additional probability
to this explanation.[25]

Objection number three. On the hypothesis
that Shakespeare was a pen-name of Bacon's this
objection, like the last, would fall to the ground,
for the essential inadequacy of the *Advancement of
Learning* in relation to poetry would explain itself
as part of the " train of secrecy." But it may also
be answered without resorting to the hypothesis.
In the *Advancement*, dramatic poesy, though
recognised, is deprived of its customary name,
" dramatic," and dubbed " representative," whilst

lyric, elegiac, and several other kinds of poetry are conspicuously ignored. The Latin version of the *Advancement*, however, the *De Augmentis Scientiarum*, published some eighteen years after the *Advancement*, not only restores to " representative poesy " its proper name " dramatic," but also mentions *elegias*, *odes*, *lyricos*, etc. The objection, as I understand it, is founded on the assumption that, at the date of the *Advancement*, Bacon had still to learn what poetry essentially was, a defect which at the date of the *De Augmentis* he had contrived to supply by getting up the subject (poetry) much as a lawyer will cram an unfamiliar subject in order to speak to his brief. But is there warrant for so questionable an assumption ? Not a scrap. To see its absurdity, one has only to compare the *Advancement of Learning* with the *Apologie for Poetry* by the " learned " Sir Philip Sidney (so the author is described on the title page), a treatise which somehow or other made its first appearance in 1595, and its second under a different title and with slight additions in 1596.[26] One of the many resemblances involved in the comparison is, not that Sidney and Bacon appear to have read the same books, but that their literary preference should have coincided so closely. Among classical authors, Plutarch was manifestly the prime favourite of both. Next after Plutarch seem to have come Virgil, Cicero, Seneca, and Ovid. The Bible, it is true, plays a far more important part in the *Advancement* than in the *Apologie*, inevitably, considering the scope of the *Advancement*, and that it was specially addressed to a theological king. In those days, however, libraries were so scantily furnished that lovers of literature necessarily became acquainted with what seems to be an unusually large proportion of the same authors.[27]   It may, therefore, be urged that similarity of literary preference did not imply direct intercommunication.   I will not argue the point, not because it is incontestable, but because there are other resemblances the cumulative force of which is more than enough for my purpose. The production of a sample half dozen of these will I hope be forgiven.   (a) According to the *Apologie for Poetrie* geometry and arithmetic would seem to be the only constituents of the science of mathematics.   The *Advancement of Learning* appears to take the same view.   (b) According to the *Apologie* " knowledge of a man's self " is the highest or " mistress " knowledge, and her highest end is " well doing and not well knowing only."   The *Advancement* holds " the end and term of natural philosophy " is " knowledge of ourselves " with a view to " active life " rather than to contemplative. (c) According to the *Apologie* "metaphysic" concerns itself with " abstract notions," builds upon " the depths of Nature " as distinct from Matter.   The *Advancement* defines " metaphysic "—which includes mathematics—as the science of " that which is abstracted and fixed," " physic " being the science of " that which is inherent in matter and therefore transitory."   (d) The *Apologie* censures philosophers for reducing " true points of knowledge " into " method " and " school art."   In the *Advancement*, Bacon condemns " the over early and peremptory reduction of knowledge into arts and methods." It is a theme on which he is ever ready to descant. Indeed, the *Novum Organum*, a congeries of aphorisms, was probably designed for a monumental warning against premature systematisation. (e) The *Apologie* contrasts the necessary limitations of other artists[28] with the perfect freedom of the poet : " only the poet . . . goeth hand in hand with nature, not inclosed within the narrow warrant of her gifts . . . where with the force of a divine breath he bringeth things forth for surpassing her doings, with no small argument to the incredulous of the first accursed fall of Adam ; sith our erected wit maketh us know what perfection is." The *Advancement*, in a charming passage, instructs us that one of the chief uses of poetry " hath been to give some shadow of satisfaction to the mind of man in those points wherein the nature of things doth deny it, the world being in proportion inferior to the soul. . . Therefore poesy was ever thought to have some participation of divineness, because it doth raise and erect the mind, by submitting the shows of things to the desires of the mind ; whereas reason doth buckle and bow the mind into the nature of things." (f) The *Apologie* holds " that there are many mysteries contained in poetry which of purpose were written darkly, lest by profane wits it should be abused." *The Advancement* affirms that one of the uses of poesy is to " retire and obscure . . . that which is delivered," " that is when the secrets and mysteries of religion, policy, and philosophy are involved in fables and parables." (g) The author of the *Apologie* venerated learning—

" the noble name of learning," he calls it—as if it were a sort of talisman. Bacon's attitude towards learning, the theme of the *Advancement*, probably differed but little, if it differed at all from that of the Apologist. (h) The aims of the two authors were to a large extent identical, for the first book of the *Advancement* was a vindication of the dignity and importance of Poetry as one of the chief constituents of " learning." Other resemblances, more or less significant, will doubtless be picked up by any alert reader. So numerous are they in the earlier portion of the *Advancement* that reading it one seems to be continually in touch with Sidney—assuming him to have been author of the *Apologie*. The effect in my own case has been such as to generate a conviction not indeed that Sidney and Bacon were personally intimate—though that is quite possible— but that Bacon when writing the *Advancement* was thoroughly familiar with the *Apologie*.

It appears then that the poetical defects or eccentricities of the *Advancement*, to whatever cause they may have been due—and honest dis- simulation is the most likely cause—were not due to ignorance of poetry. Consequently the last of the three objections fails of effect.

" But," says one, " suppose for a moment that your precious theory is not incoherent, what then ? A dream is not less a dream because it happens to hang together. So with your theory. Its value is of the smallest unless it serve to harmonise or explain phenomena otherwise intractable. The omission to apply this test is fatal to your pretensions." I have no fault to find with the criticism, except that it is founded on misapprehension. It takes for granted that I have undertaken to establish something, a Bacon theory to wit. That feat may be possible to an able advocate, after a " harvest of new disclosures." For my part, so diffident am I of my power to do anything of the kind, that the thought of attempting it here had not even occurred to me.

For the rest, on good cause shown my precious theory will be abandoned without reserve and without a pang, though I shall hardly be able to rise to that fullness of joy which according to M. Poincaré (Le Science et l'Hypothèse) ought to be felt by the physicist who has just renounced a favourite hypothesis because it has failed to satisfy a crucial test.

NOTES TO SHAKESPEARE—A THEORY

(1) Note : The words philosopher, philosophy, philosophicals throughout this paper mean what they meant in Bacon's day. The word science, on the other hand, when not in quotation, is to be understood in its modern sense.

(2) From Sidney's *Apologie for Poetrie* (of which more hereafter) we learn that he was in the secret of some " *Queis meliore luto finxit præcordia Titan*, and who are better content to suppress the outflowing of their wit than by publishing it to be accounted knights of the same order " as those " servile wits who think it enough to be rewarded of the printer." Similarly Puttenham, in his *Arte of English Poesie* (1589), writes : " I know very many notable Gentlemen in the Court that have written commendably and suppressed it again, or else suffered it to be publisht without their names to it." The *Arte of English Poesie* was dedicated to Bacon's uncle and *quasi* guardian, Lord Burleigh. In this connexion, a saying ascribed to Edmund Waller is worth notice : " Sidney and Bacon were nightingales who sang only in the spring, it was the diversion of their youth."

SHAKESPEARE—A THEORY

(3) From Mr. Shakespeare's autographs one gathers that he was indifferent as to the spelling of his name, and that if he had a preference, it was for the form Shakspere rather than Shakespeare. For my present purpose it is necessary to distinguish between the owner of New Place, Stratford, and the author of Macbeth and Lear. For the former, Shakspere would have been better than " Mr. Shakespeare." But having followed the Belvoir document so far, I shall continue to use " Mr." as the distinction between the two—without prejudice to the question whether or not they were actually one and the same. [The signatures show that the Stratford player wrote his name " Shakspere." He seems never to have made use of the form " Shakespeare," which is, in truth, a quite different name from that of " Shakspere," or " Shaksper," or " Shaxpur," and such like forms. Ed.]

(4) Some will have it that Shakespeare was a kind of writing machine, and look to Ben Jonson as their prophet. Yet Jonson's testimony both in the great Ode to Shakespeare and elsewhere—agreeing herein with the internal evidence of several of the plays—negatives a mechanical explanation.

(5) In the case of something which apparently " grew from " himself, dealt with the Deposing of Richard II, and " went about in other men's names," pseudonymity seems to have failed to screen Bacon from cross-examination and censure by Queen Elizabeth. (Bacon's *Apologie in certaine imputations concerning the late Earl of Essex*. 1604.)

(6) Browning and others less eminent than he have questioned the autobiographical value of the *Sonnets*. Even so they would be serious *impedimenta* to a Solicitor-General on his way to the Attorney-Generalship, Privy Councillorship, and other conspicuous offices.

(7) It is obviously borrowed, *mutatis mutandis*, from Ovid's *Metamorphoses*. " Deeper than did ever plummet sound," however, is not from Ovid's *Medea*, but it seems to me from Act III, Sc. 3, of *The Tempest* itself. Golding's English version of the *Metamorphoses* may well have been in the writer's mind along with the Latin original.

(8) *Advancement of Learning*. " Art of · Arts " was a favourite phrase of his. Of " rational knowledges " he says in the same book : " These be truly said to be the art of arts."

(9)   The *idée mère* of the *Sapientia Veterum*—allegorisation—is one which I think no notable man of science among his contemporaries would have attempted to press into the service of science as Bacon pressed it.   With contemporary men of letters, poets especially, it was in high favour, partly I suppose as an exercise of ingenuity, partly as a " talking point " wherewith to capture the vulgar, and partly of course for higher reasons. Sir John Harington's application of it to *Orlando Furioso* (1591), is a *reductio ad absurdum* of the fashion.

(10)   Poetry for example !

(11)   The second book of the *Advancement*—where " rational knowledges " or " arts intellectual " are being discussed—promises, " if God give me leave, a disquisition, digested into two parts ; whereof the one I term *experientia literata*, and the other *interpretatio naturæ*, the former being but a degree or rudiment of the latter." What the latter was in 1605 is matter of conjecture.   Possibly *Valerius Terminus, Of the Interpretation of Nature, with the Annotations of Hermes Stella*, a curious essay, seemingly meant to be anonymous, or pseudonymous, may enable us to measure its value.   Concerning the former, *experientia literata*, we may learn from the *De Augmentis Scientiarum*, the authorised Latin version of the *Advancement of Learning*, quite as much as any of us need wish to know.
It may be well to bear in mind that in addition to the above double promise, the *Advancement of Learning* contains other promises including one, " if God give me leave," of a legal work —*prudentia activa*—digested into aphorisms.

(12)   The nebulous *Temporis Partus Maximus*, of very uncertain date, was scarcely more serious, I suppose, than the eloquent eulogies of " knowledge " or " philosophy " in Bacon's " apparently unacknowledged " *Conference of Pleasure*, 1592, and *Gesta Graiorum*, 1594, though towards the close of his life he seems to have claimed for it a somewhat higher value.

(13)   According to Professor Fowler (*Francis Bacon*, Macmillan) the foundation of the Royal Society was due to the impulse given by Bacon to experimental science.   Dr. Abbott (*Francis Bacon*, Macmillan) is struck by a different aspect of Bacon : " By a strange irony the great depreciator of words seems destined to derive an immortal memory from the rich variety of his style and the vastness of his too sanguine expectations."   I cannot help doubting whether, if Bacon had died before 1620 or thereabouts, he would have been held to have placed experimental science under any obligation at all.

(14)   No student I suppose would willingly be without the volume here quoted, " *Francis Bacon*, by Edwin A. Abbott.

(15)   Rawley's dedication, 1627, of the *Natural History* to Charles the First.

(16)   *Advancement of Learning.*   Book I.

(17)   The art of prolonging life was, he thought, one of the most desirable.

(18)   He " bequeathed " his soul and body to God.   " For my name and memory I leave it to men's charitable speeches, and to foreign nations, and to the next ages."

(19)   Rawley in the dedication of 1627 uses this expression as if it were Bacon's rather than his own.

(20)   I am not aware that in its integrity it is shared by anyone.

(21)   More easily by far than Mr. Shakespeare's neglect of his supposed poetical issue more especially after his retirement to Stratford.   What was there, what would there be in the Stratford of those days with its Quineys, Harts, Sadlers, Walkers, and the rest, to interest a spirit so finely touched as Shakespeare's ?   But this is too large a question to be discussed here.

(22)   James I is reported to have said of the *Novum Organum* : " It is like the peace of God which passeth all understanding."

(23)   Bacon's tripartite division of knowledge history with memory for its organ, poetry with imagination, and philosophy with reason—is well known.   When he made this division the poetic use of the imagination was one which few may have known better than he.   That he was equally well acquainted with the scientific use of the imagination is highly improbable.

(24)   Sir P. Sidney seems to have arrived at a like conclusion, for he speaks of an " honest dissimulation."

(25)   Whether the absence of proof that Bacon, as Dr. Abbott observes, " felt any pride in or set any value on his unique mastery of English " should be similarly interpreted is a more difficult question.   Possibly admiration of his vernacular became nauseous to him as suggesting something less than admiration

of his philosophy. Of his Latin, the Latin of the *Sapientia Veterum*, he writes to his friend : "They tell me my Latin is turned silver and become current." His apparent indifference to vehicle or language therefore did not extend beyond his mother tongue.

(26) It must have circulated privately some years before 1595, for Sir John Harington in his English version (1591) of Ariosto's *Orlando Furioso*, calls Sidney " our English Petrarke," and refers to his *Apologie for Poetry* (along with the *Arte of English Poesie*, 1589, dedicated to Lord Burleigh) as handling sundry poetical questions " right learnedly." I may add that the motto to Sidney's *Apologie—odi profanum vulgus et arceo—* touches the motto to Shakespeare's *Venus and Adonis* ; that *King Lear* touches the *Arcadia* ; and generally that a complete enumeration of the apparent contacts between Sidney and Shakespeare would probably fill many pages. [Some have even ventured to doubt whether the poetry which goes in the name of Sidney, who died at Zutphen in 1586, was really written by Sidney at all. Ed.]

(27) It is interesting to note in relation to Aristotle, who is cited again and again in both *Advancement* and *Apologie*, that the *Apologie* endorses his dramatic precept of " one place, one day." Another of the *Apologie's* references to Aristotle : " which reason of his, as all his, is most full of reason," gives one to think. The *Advancement* disapproves, it may be added, of tying modern tongues to ancient measures : " In modern languages it seemeth to me as free to make new measures of verses as of dances."

(28) Astronomy and metaphysic are there considered as *arts*, whilst poetry ranks as a *science*.

BEN JONSON AND SHAKESPEARE

BEN JONSON AND SHAKESPEARE*

ANOTHER exasperating lucubration on the Shakespeare problem! We have the Plays themselves. Why disturb a venerable belief by hypotheses incapable of proof, and neither venerable nor even respectable? To answer offhand—Curiosity about the *How* of remarkable events is not likely to die out so long as intelligent beings continue to exist : Without the aid of hypotheses, science were impossible : Astronomers would still be expounding the once venerated doctrine of a stable Earth and a revolving Sun, a doctrine daily corroborated by the testimony of our eyes. Moreover, the " venerable belief " that Shakspere and Shakespeare were one and the same is mainly founded on the hypothesis that Ben Jonson's famous Ode to Shakespeare (1623) is all to be taken at face-value. Praise—splendid praise —is unquestionably its dominant constituent ; but other ingredients—enigma, jest, *make-believe*—are commingled with the praise.

The exordium of this Ode consists of sixteen laborious lines :

> To draw no envy (Shakespeare) on thy name,
> Am I thus ample to thy Booke and Fame ;
> While I confesse thy writings to be such,
> As neither Man nor Muse can praise too much.

* This Essay was written by Mr. Smithson in the year 1919.

Tis true, and all mens suffrage. But these wayes
  Were not the paths I meant unto thy praise ;
For seeliest Ignorance on these may light,
  Which, when it sounds at best, but eccho's right ;
Or blinde Affection, which doth ne'er advance
  The truth, but gropes, and urgeth all by chance ;
Or crafty Malice might pretend this praise,
  And thinke to ruine, where it seem'd to raise.
These are, as some infamous Baud, or whore,
  Should praise a Matron. What could hurt her more ?
But thou art proof against them, and indeed
  Above th'ill fortune of them, or the need.
I, therefore, will begin, etc.

This emphatic disclaimer of any intention to
draw envy, ill-will, discredit, on the august name
Shakespeare, had a deep meaning, or Jonson would
not have given it such prominence. It reads as
if addressed to a living person, and the subsequent
apostrophe, " Thou art a Moniment, without a
tombe," chimes with this suggestion. The root
difficulty of the passage lies in the obviously genuine
conviction of the author that Shakespeare was in
danger of being hurt by praise, noble, sincere and
universally allowed to be just. As for the assertion
that Shakespeare was " indeed above " the reach
of harm, it is only pretence. Having dispatched
this tiresome business, the eulogist lets himself
go :

I therefore will begin, Soule of the Age !
  The applause ! delight ! the wonder of our Stage !
My Shakespeare, rise ; I will not lodge thee by
  Chaucer, or Spenser, or bid Beaumont lye
A little further, to make thee a roome ,
  Thou art a Moniment, without a tombe.
        *   *   *   *
And though thou hadst small Latine, and lesse Greeke,
  From thence to honour thee, I would not seeke
For names ; but call forth thund'ring Aeschilus,
  Euripides, and Sophocles to us,

BEN JONSON AND SHAKESPEARE

Paccuvius, Accius, him of Cordova dead,
  To life againe, to heare thy buskin tread,
And shake a Stage ; Or, when thy Sockes were on,
  Leave thee alone, for the comparison
Of all that insolent Greece, or haughtie Rome
  Sent forth, or since did from their ashes come.
Triumph, my Britaine, thou hast one to showe,
  To whom all scenes of Europe homage owe.
He was not of an age, but for all time !
  And all the Muses still were in their prime,
When like Apollo he came forth to warme
  Our eares, or like a Mercury to charme.
Nature herselfe was proud of his designes,
  And joy'd to weare the dressing of his lines.

. . . . Looke how the fathers face
  Lives in his issue, even so, the race
Of Shakespeares minde, and manners brightly shines
  In his well turned, and true-filed lines ;
In each of which, he seems to shake a Lance,
  As brandish't at the eyes of ignorance.
Sweet Swan of Avon ! What a sight it were
  To see thee in our waters yet appeare,
And make those flights upon the bankes of Thames,
  That so did take Eliza and our James.
But stay. I see thee in the Hemisphere
  Advanc'd, and made a Constellation there.
Shine forth, thou Starre of Poets, and with rage,
  Or Influence, chide, or cheere the drooping Stage ;
Which since thy flight fro' hence, hath mourn'd like night,
  And despaires day, but by thy Volumes Light."

Passing by the half serious " Thou art a Moniment without a tombe," we are pulled up by the line: " And though thou hadst small Latine," etc. The internal evidence of his poems and plays proves that Shakespeare must have had a regular education, as distinguished from mere smatterings picked up in a village school of the sixteenth century. As to Latin in particular, the etymological intelligence shown in the handling of words derived from that language is almost conclusive. The evidence of contemporaries tells the same tale. "W.C.," for instance, in *Polimanteia* (c. 1595) intimates that Shakespeare was a "schollar," and a member of one of our "Universities."* But there is no need to labour the point of Shakespeare's culture. Indeed the innuendo of " small Latin " as applied to Shakespeare is sufficiently refuted by other passages in the Ode itself. "All scenes of Europe," classico-historical as well as modern, owe him "homage." He was another " Apollo "; each of his " well turned and true-filed lines " was sufficient to enlighten " ignorance." What then are we to make of a jibe, apparently levelled at Shakespeare, that he was a quite unlettered rustic? Some years after the date of the Ode, and in order, as he says, to justify his " owne candor," Jonson told " posterity " (as we shall see) that Shakespeare wrote with a " facility " so unbridled that he often blundered.† But even then, though his mood in the interval had veered right round from eulogist to candid critic, Jonson dropped no hint that Shakespeare lacked Latin or Greek. The jibe therefore, did not fit Shakespeare, but must have been made to the measure of some one else.

To continue our examination of the Ode. What can Jonson have meant by interspersing it with trashy jests upon the two syllables of the name (no longer august) Shakespeare? " Shake a stage "; " shake a lance, as brandished at the eyes of

---

* See my *Shakespeare Problem Restated*, p. 342. [Ed.]

† Jonson says " wherein he flowed with that facility that sometimes it was necessary he should be stop'd ; *Sufflaminandus erat*, as Augustus said of Haterius." This means that he had to be " stop'd " not in *writing* but in *talking*. See my *Is there a Shakespeare Problem?* p. 386, *seq.* [Ed.]

ignorance." Was there something irresistibly funny about the name? Again, what sort of ignorance was threatened by the beauty and finish of Shakespeare's lines? The ignorance of persons who for Shakespeare mistook a man untinctured with literature? The " Sweet Swan of Avon " apostrophe suggests comparison with what, in his *Masque of Owles* (1626), Jonson wrote about "Warwick Muses." These charming creatures are there represented as inspired, not by "Pegasus," but by a " Hoby-horse."* Was this sarcasm reminiscent of the well-known lines which an Oxford graduate informs us were " oɪdered " by the Strattord man " to be cut upon his tombstone " ? Certainly Pegasus was innocent of them. Here they are :

> Good frend, for Jesus sake forbeare
> To digg the dust encloased heare ;
> Bleste be the man that spares these stones,
> And curst be he that moves my bones.

To return to the Ode. The lines which follow the " Sweet Swan " apostrophe are deserving of notice, chiefly because they tell us that King James (as well as Queen Elizabeth) was under the spell of Shakespeare. Then comes the ejaculation : " But stay ! I see thee in the hemisphere advanced, and made a constellation there." Is it possible that Jonson expected his readers—such of them as were not in the secret—to follow him here ? To

---

* The so-called *Masque of Owls* begins with the stage-direction : " Enter Captain Cox on his Hobby horse," of which animal the Captain says : " He is the Pegasus that uses to wait on Warwick Muses, and on gaudy days he paces Before the Coventry Graces." The " Warwick Muses " are generally supposed to be the Morris-dancers of the county, with whom the hobby-horse was usually associated. [Ed.]

behold Shakespeare, *à la* Berenice's hair, translated into the constellation Cygnus ? Not he ; that were an order too large for credulity itself to honour. What Jonson had in his mind's eye was not the starry heaven, but the British House of Peers.* Such is this famous Ode. It suffers from manœuvres, the object of which had to be kept dark ; and this I take to be the reason for its exclusion from the second volume (1640) of Jonson's Works, where it would have been quite at home amongst the Odes, Sonnets, Elegies and so forth, which go to make up that volume.

Turn we now to Jonson's *Timber* or *Discoveries*, a work written years after the Ode and not printed till 1641, some three or four years after his death. These *Discoveries* consist in the main of passages lifted from Latin writers, notably Seneca the father (*Controversiæ*), and entered promiscuously in Jonson's Commonplace books. The borrowings are often mutilated and always treated without ceremony. For our purpose it is the application, not the accuracy of translation that matters. In quoting from them I shall give italics and capital letters as they appear in the slovenly print (1641), of which I have several copies, one of which by the way is inscribed " J. P. Collier " on the title page. A *Discovery* concerning Poets, runs thus :

> Nothing in our Age, I have observed, is more pre-posterous, than the *running Judgments* upon *Poetry* and *Poets ;* when we shall heare those things . . . cried up for the best writings, which a man would scarce vouchsafe to wrap any wholesome drug in ; he would

* To which, of course, Bacon had been " translated," first as Baron Verulam, and later as Viscount St. Alban. [Ed.]

never light his *Tobacco* with them. . . . There are
never wanting, that dare preferre the worst . . . *Poets :*
. . . Nay, if it were put to the question of the Water-
rimers workes, against Spencer's, I doubt not but they
[the Water-rimers'] would find more suffrages.

The next *Discovery* is more to my purpose :

> *Poetry* in this latter Age, hath prov'd but a meane
> *Mistresse* to such as have wholly addicted themselves
> to her ; or given their names up to her family. They
> who have but saluted her on the by, and now and then
> tendred their visits, shee hath done much for, and
> advanced in the way of their owne professions (both the
> *Law* and the *Gospel*) beyond all they could have hoped or
> done for themselves without her favour.

From this the reader will gather that under
" Eliza and our James," lawyer-poets who masked
their poems—" in a players hide," perhaps—were
likely candidates for legal honours.

The next *Discovery* but one runs thus :

> *De Shakespeare nostrat.* I remember the players have
> often mentioned it as an honour to Shakespeare, that in
> all his writing (whatever he penned) hee never blotted
> out a line. My answer hath beene, would he had blotted
> a thousand. . . . I had not told posterity this, but for
> their ignorance who chose that circumstance to commend
> their friend by wherein he most faulted. And to justifie
> mine owne candor, for I lov'd the man and doe honour
> his memory (on this side idolatry) as much as any. He
> was indeed honest, and of an open and free nature ;
> had excellent phantasie ; brave notions and gentle
> expressions ; wherein he flow'd with that facility that
> sometime it was necessary he should be stop'd. . . .
> His wit was in his owne power, would the rule of it had
> beene so too. . . . But he redeemed his vices with
> his vertues.

Another *Discovery* (p. 99)* censures " all the
Essayists, even their Master *Montaigne*." The

* This is No. LXV. Nota 6, in Sir I. Gollancz's Edition. [Ed.]

BACONIAN ESSAYS

slur suggested by this censure upon Bacon is significant. We were wont to believe that Bacon's fame as a master of English rested securely on his *Essays*, and perhaps among his *acknowledged* works no better foundation is discoverable. Jonson's estimate (to be quoted presently) of Bacon's achievement " in our tongue," is at least as high as ours. Yet Jonson does not appreciate Bacon's *Essays*. The dilemma seems to be this : either Jonson was writing at random, or he knew of unacknowledged Baconian work which he was not free to disclose.

Another *Discovery* treats *De claris Oratoribus*, and among them of *Dominus Verulamius** in these words :

> There hapn'd in my time one noble *Speaker*, who was full of gravity in his speaking. His language (where hee could spare or passe by a jest) was nobly *censorious*. . . . No member of his speech but consisted of his owne graces. His hearers could not cough, or looke aside from him, without losse. . . . No man had their affections more in his power. The feare of every man that heard him was lest hee should make an end.

On the next page after an appreciative notice of the *De Augmentis Scientiarum*, which was published almost simultaneously with the Shakespeare Ode, Jonson over-praises and misreads the *Novum Organum* in these words :

> Which though by most of superficiall men, who cannot get beyond the Title of *Nominals*, it is not penetrated, nor understood ; it really openeth all defects of Learning whatsoever and is a Booke ; *Qui longum noto scriptori porriget ævum.*

* No. LXXI.

BEN JONSON AND SHAKESPEARE

My object in giving these two quotations is only to show that there is nothing in them to lead up to the arresting praise of Bacon expressed in my next quotation, which comes after a list of English writers or *wits*, the elder *Wiat*, the *Earl of Surrey*, Sir *Philip Sidney* (a " great Master of wit,") *Lord Egerton*, the Chancellor, and runs thus :

> But his [the *his* refers to L. C. Egerton] learned and able, though unfortunate *Successor*, is he, who hath fill'd up all numbers, and perform'd that in our tongue, which may be compar'd, or preferr'd, either to insolent *Greece*, or haughty *Rome*. In short, within his view, and about his times, were all the wits borne, that could honour a language, or help study. Now things daily fall ; wits grow downe-ward, and *Eloquence* growes back-ward : So that hee may be nam'd, and stand as the *marke* and *akme* of our language.*

In order to appreciate this passage, the reader should grasp (1) that Jonson's mind at the time was full of memories of Bacon ; (2) that in a subsequent Discovery—*De Poetica*—he distinguishes *Poetry* from oratory as " the most prevailing," " most exalted " " Eloquence," and describes the Poet's " skill or Craft of making " as the " Queene of Arts " ; (3) that Jonson, proud of his own *métier* as poet, would never have allowed, still less asserted, that Bacon had " filled up all numbers," had he not known that Bacon was a great poet. Where is this wonderful poetry to be found ? The answer is ready to hand. The famous writer who, according to the *Discovery*, had " perform'd that in our tongue " which neither Greece nor Rome could surpass, is the very man who, according to the Ode, had achieved that in *English* which defied

* No. LXXII.

" comparison " with " all " that Greece or Rome, or the civilisations that succeeded Greece and Rome, had given to the World. Bacon is that Man, and Shakespeare was his pen-name.

This hypothesis—that Shakespeare was the pen-name of Bacon—will pilot us through our difficulties. The disclaimer (in the Ode) for example, of any intention to injure the august name need puzzle us no longer. Bacon's reputation was imperilled by publication of the great Book ; for if the Public once got wind that he had trafficked with " common players " his name, already smirched by the verdict of the House of Peers, would have been irreparably damaged. A passage from an anonymous Essay of mine (*Bacon-Shakespeare* ; projected 1884-5 : published 1899), may be tolerated here. The Essay, after having suggested that Greene's allusion to Shakespeare as having a " tiger's heart wrapt in a player's hide " pointed to concealment behind an actor, proceeds :

> John Davies . . . characterises poetry (contemporaneous) as " a worke of darkness," in the sense of a secret work, not in disparagement : Davies loved poetry and poets too well for that. The anonymous author of *Wit's Recreations*, in a kindly epigram " To Mr. William Shake-speare," says : " Shake-speare we must be silent in thy praise, cause our encomions will but blast thy bayes." . . . Edward Bolton in the . . . sketch (or draft) of his *Hypercritica*, . . . after having mentioned " Shakespeare, Beaumont, and other writers for the stage " thinks it necessary to remind himself that their names required to be " tenderly used in this argument." (accordingly) He . . . excluded the name of Shakespeare . . . from the published version of his *Hypercritica*.

To return again to the Ode. Its jests about shaking a stage (compare Greene's " Shakescene "), shaking a lance, and its ecstatic vision of Shakespeare enthroned among the stars were no doubt intended to amuse the two Earls, and other patrons of the famous Folio.

As for the sweeping accusation in the *Timber* or *Discoveries*, that Poetry had been a mean Mistress to openly professed as distinguished from furtive or concealed poets, it would have been unpardonable had the Stratford man been a poet ; for William Shakspere, Esq., of New Place, Stratford-on-Avon, spent his last years in the odour of prosperity.

Other testimony, quite independent of Jonson's, to the existence of an intimate relation between Bacon and the Muses, Apollo, Helicon, Parnassus, is abundant enough. Here are a few samples : Thomas Randolph shortly after Bacon's death accuses Phœbus of being accessory to Bacon's death, lest the God himself should be dethroned and Bacon be crowned king of the Muses.* George Herbert calls Bacon the colleague of Apollo. Thomas Campion, addressing Bacon says : "Whether . . . the Law, or the Schools (in the sense of science or knowledge), or the sweet Muse allure thee," etc. At a somewhat later date, Waller said that Bacon and Sidney were nightingales who sang only in the spring (the reference has escaped me, and memory may possibly deceive me).† Coming to comparatively recent times we find Shelley, an exceptional judge of poetry, was of

---

* See *Manes Verulamiani*, published by Sir Wm. Rawley (1626). No. 32, by Thomas Randolph of Trinity College, Cambridge. [Ed.]

† Waller in the dedication of his works to Queen Henrietta Maria, speaks of Sir Philip Sidney and Sir Francis Bacon as " Nightingales who sang only with spring ; it was the diversion of their youth." [ED.]

opinion that Bacon "was a poet." It may possibly be objected that Bacon's versified Psalms (in English) are not poetical.* But these Psalms belong to about 1624, when Bacon—*ex hypothesi*—had turned his back on poetry for ever. What they prove, if they prove anything, is that Bacon was a literary Proteus who could take on any disguise that happened to suit his purpose, a faculty which no student of Bacon would ever think of disputing.

Inferences drawn from Bacon's reticence or extracted from his works have yet to be weighed. In the nineties of the sixteenth century he can be shown to have devoted much time and thought to the writing and preparation of a species of dramatic entertainment known as *Devices*. Even after he became Lord Chancellor, he risked injuring his health rather than deny himself the pleasure of assisting at a dramatic performance given by Gray's Inn. As a student of human nature, moreover, he had scarcely an equal (bar " Shakespeare.") And yet he seems to have been ignorant of the existence of any such person as Shakespeare, although that name must have been bandied about and about in the London of his day, especially among members of the various Inns of Court, his own Gray's in particular.

Neglecting Bacon's poetical and interesting *Devices*, I confine my observations to the *Advancement of Learning* (1605), which though not written in what Waller held to be the singing time of life, reveals (while trying to conceal) the true bent of his genius. The Work was expressly intended to

* See note *ante* p. 84. [Ed.]

embrace the totality of human knowledge then garnered. Yet with the air of one who had no misgivings about the propriety of his classification he divides his vast subject into three categories, three only, and one of these is *Poesie*. The other two are *History* and *Philosophie*, the latter of which embraces " Natural Science," divided into " Phisicke " and " Metaphisicke," " Mathematicke" pure and mixt, anatomy, medicine, mental and moral science, and much besides. The work teems with poetical quotations, similies, allusions. Dealing with medicine the author gravely informs his readers that " the poets did well to conjoin music and medicine in Apollo, because the office of medicine is but to tune this curious harp of man's body, and reduce it to harmony." He cannot refrain from telling us that the pseudo-science of the alchemist was foretold and discredited by the fable of Ixion and the Cloud. With him, what we mean by endowment of research becomes provision for encouraging " experiments appertaining to Vulcan and Dædalus," etc. No wonder the Harveys, Napiers, and other pioneers of 17th. century science did not join in that chorus of admiration for Bacon, which seems to have included all 17th century men of letters. Sir Henry Wotton (for example) will have it that Bacon had " done a great and ever living benefit to all the children of Nature ; and to Nature herself in her uttermost extent . . . who never before had so noble nor so true an interpreter, or so inward a secretary of her cabinet." One can imagine the laughter with which Galileo would have greeted this preposterous assertion.

Out of sight of philosophy, metaphysics, mathematics, etc., and in the presence of poetry, the author is in his element and speaks with authority. In handling the subject of mental culture—" Georgics of the mind " is his phrase— he takes for granted that poets (with whom he couples historians) are the best teachers of this science, for in them :

> We may find painted forth, how affections are kindled and incited ; and how pacified and refrained ; and how again contained from act and further degree ; how they disclose themselves ; how they work ; how they vary ; how they gather and fortify ; how they are enwrapped one within another ; and how they do fight and encounter one with another.

" Poesie," he says elsewhere, is " for the most part restrained in measure of words," but in " other points extreamely licensed, and doth truly refer to the imagination." Its use, he goes on to say :

> Hath been to give some shadow of satisfaction to the mind of man in those points wherein the nature of things doth deny it, the world being in proportion inferior to the soul ; by reason whereof there is agreeable to the spirit of man, a more ample greatness, a more exact goodness, and a more absolute variety, than can be found in the nature of things . . . and therefore it was ever thought to have some participation of divineness, because it doth raise and erect the mind, by submitting the shows of things to the desires of the mind. . . . In this third part of learning (or knowledge) which is poesie, I can report no deficience. For being as a plant that cometh of the lust of the earth, without formal seed, it hath sprung up and spread abroad more than any other kind. But to ascribe unto it that which is due ; for the expressing of affections, passions, corruptions, and customs, we are beholding to poets more than to the philosophers' works ;

and for wit and eloquence, not much less than to orators'
harangues. But it is not good to stay too long in the
theatre.

Why, when he was enumerating the various kinds
of poesie, did he eschew the apt word *dramatic*,
and choose the vague word *representative* instead ?
Why hurry away from his subject (poetry) by reason
of its intimate connection with the *theatre* ? The
answer leaps to the eye.   For him, poetry, especially
dramatic poetry, was like (the name) Shakespeare,
under taboo.

The Bacon hypothesis, it may be urged, solves a
few riddles.   But what of the difficulties it involves ?
For example, it seems incredible that Bacon should
ever have resolved to disown his wonderful
offspring ;   except indeed on the impossible
assumption that he, with his unrivalled knowledge
of human nature and command of all the arts of
expression—that he of all men was incapable of
appreciating the children of his brain.   Here, once
more, my anonymous Essay suggests pertinent
considerations :

> The emotional chill, which rarely fails to accompany
> that creeping illness, old age, was one of these con-
> siderations. Another was the growth of a widespread
> feeling . . . that English books would never be
> " citizens of the world," that Latin was the " universal
> language" and Latin books the only books that " would
> live." But there must have been a " strain of rareness "
> about Shakespeare's affection for poetry, which nothing
> but a new and incompatible emotion could ever have
> subdued. . . . With Bacon, affection for literature,
> especially poetry, came (in time) long before affection
> for anything like science. Among the various indications
> of this, not the least interesting is a passage in the *De
> Augmentis Scientiarum* (the latinised version, 1623, of
> the more noteworthy *Advancement of Learning*, 1605,

already quoted):—" Poesy is at it were a dream of learning; a thing sweet and varied and fain to be thought partly divine, a quality which dreams also sometimes affect. But now it is time for me to become fully awake, to lift myself up from the earth, and to wing my way through the liquid ether of philosophy and the sciences." Of a certainty this beautiful passage was no mere flourish. . . . It was a pathetic renunciation—the last possibly of a series of more or less ineffectual renunciations—of poetry and an . . . aspiration after something else, neither poetry, nor science, nor philosophy, which Bacon towards the close of life was wont to regard, so Rawley informs us, as " his darling philosophy."

In other words, the *Novum Organum*, the potent *New Instrument* that was to enlarge man's dominion over every province of Nature, was Bacon's chief solace for an unparalleled renunciation. Posterity, he was determined, should never know that the inventor of that *Instrument* had once revelled in the play of the imagination, lest men of science should have it in their power to pooh-pooh it as the fabric of a brain that had invented *A Midsummer-night's Dream*, and *The Tempest*.

Bacon and his friends (moved by the fascination of the man, and pity for his fall) would naturally destroy all tell-tale correspondence they could lay hands on. Two private letters, and so far as we know, two only, escaped the flames. One from a bosom friend, Sir T. Mathew to Bacon (" Viscount St. Alban "), bears the following postscript : " The most prodigious wit that ever I knew of my nation . . . is of your Lordship's name, though he be known by another." This letter is given in Dr. Birch's *Letters, etc., of Francis Bacon*, 1763. Mathew himself made a *Collection of Letters* which included many of his own to Bacon, but excluded the one just quoted, an exclusion dictated, I imagine, by loyalty to his friend. Montague gives the letter in his *Bacon*, but I have not found it in Spedding's Work. The other escape was a letter of Bacon's to another of his friends, the poet Davies, written some twenty years earlier than Mathew's letter. In this letter (to Davies), after commending himself to Davies's "love," and "the well using of my name . . . if there be any biting or nibling at it, in that place " (the Royal Court), Bacon concludes : " So desiring you to be good to concealed poets, I continue," etc. My quotation is from a copy dated 1657 (bound up with Rawley's *Resuscitatio*), in which " concealed poets " is in italics. Spedding gives the words without the italics, and contents himself with saying that he cannot explain them. For another letting cut of the secret we have to thank Aubrey's notebooks, which inform us that Bacon was " a good poet but concealed, as appears by his letters." Lastly there are the " Shakespeare " and " Bacon " scribbles on the half-burnt MS. of Bacon's " Device," *A Conference of Pleasure*. Possibly the " letters " referred to by Aubrey, or evidence more important, may yet be discovered in libraries unexplored, or explored only by orthodox searchers intent on proving their own case. A library in so unlikely a place as Valladolid seems, about eighty years ago, to have possessed a First Folio of Shakespeare which belonged to and was perhaps annotated by Count Gondomar, a friend of Bacon's last years.*

* Mrs. Humphry Ward's *Reminiscences*, 1918, are, if memory fail not, my authority here. [See Mrs. H. Ward's *Recollections*, pp. 255-258, and an interesting letter, headed " Shakespeare Folios," and signed " A. R. Watson," in *The Times* of April 13, 1922. Ed.]

If Spain held such a treasure so recently what may not Great Britain still hold ? Florence, for whose Duke Sir T. Mathew had Bacon's *Essays* translated into Italian, contained a copy of this translation not long ago. But my searches there, and in Venice, Milan, Padua, were far too hurried to justify any conclusion as to possible finds in Italy.

It is probably safe to take for granted that Bacon was acquainted with Shakspere ; that the relation between them began maybe as early as 1588, and was concerned with playhouse property ; that this property was held by Shakspere on trust for Bacon ; and that it was sold, perhaps to the trustees, by Bacon's orders some time before 1613.

The name of " Shakespeare " seems to have made its first public appearance in print with *Venus and Adonis,** a poem which was dedicated in perfectly well-bred terms to an earl ; licensed by an archbishop who had once been Bacon's tutor ;† and expressed on its title page patrician contempt for all things vulgar. By whose order was the name Shakespeare printed at foot of its Dedication to the Earl of Southampton ? In the dearth of evidence the following guesses may pass muster. They are put into an unhistorical present

---

*It cannot be proved that Shakspere ever spelt his name Shakespeare. Shakspere seems to be the form he preferred. Probably however, both he and his illiterate father Shaxper, Shaksper, Shakspear, or what not, were anything but fastidious about spellings. Persons who happen to be interested in the Shakspere family's fifty or sixty ways of spelling their name will thank me for referring them to Sir George Greenwood's *Shakespeare Problem* where they will find it stated that " the form Shakespeare seems never to have been employed by them." Among examples of destructive criticism of the Stratford theory, I know not one so exhaustive and deadly as this of Sir G. Greenwood's. In my *Shakespeare-Bacon Essay*, Shakspere, his irredeemably vulgar Will, and other doings, are relegated to an appendix.

†Whitgift to wit. [Ed.]

in order to show at a glance that they, or most of them, are mere guess-work :—About 1592, Bacon makes up his mind to publish *Venus and Adonis*. Publication in his own name is vetoed by fear of offending powerful friends, his uncle Burghley in particular ; and he prefers pseudonymity to anonymity. What he wants is a temporary mask which he fully expects to be able to throw off before long. In this mood, he calls on Richard Field, a London printer hailing originally from Stratford, and recommended to him by Sir John Harington, whose *Orlando Furioso* Field has just printed. Field happens to mention Shakspere which he pronounces Shaxper. Bacon, already acquainted with the young fellow of that name, decides that a fictitious person, whose name he pronounces Shake-speare, shall be the putative father of his Poem. Little dreams he, poet though he be, that he is thereby preparing a human grave for that im-mortality of Fame (as poet) which he has begun to anticipate for himself. The Poem appears in 1593 ; and is followed next year by *Lucrece*, fathered by the same Shakespeare, and dedicated to the same young Earl. Some years later, the name is stereotyped by Meres's *Commonwealth of Wits*, where Shakespeare is mentioned seven or eight times—as the English Ovid ; as one of our best tragic and best comic poets ; as one of our most " wittie " and accomplished writers, and so forth.*
A few years later still, Bacon begins to be perplexed what to do with his Shakespeare copyright, and his perplexity rises with every advance in his profession.

* The allusion is to Francis Meres's *Palladis Tamia*, 1598. [Ed.]

Before succeeding to the Attorney-Generalship he realises once for all that complications, professional, social, and various, have made it impossible for him to think of fathering even a selection of his poetical offspring. In despair to escape from the impasse, he even talks of burning MSS. But the threat is not carried out. Soon after his melancholy downfall sympathetic and admiring friends, notably the two Earls of Pembroke and Montgomery—Southampton probably stood aloof, memories of the Essex affair still rankling in his mind—take counsel together, expostulate with him, entreat him to let them bear all expenses and responsibilities connected with publication, and to clinch their argument tell him that they have sounded the literary dictator of the day, Ben Jonson, and got his promise to undertake the work of editing, collecting, writing the necessary prefatory matter, and so forth. Bacon yields consent on certain conditions, the most embarrassing of which is that the true authorship of the plays be for ever kept dark—by means of " dissimulation," if dissimulation will serve ; if not, then by " simulation," i.e., the lie direct.* The conditions are accepted with misgivings on Jonson's part. He is aware that he will have no trouble with Mr. Shakspere's executors, their interest in the copyrights involved being as negligible as their testator's had been. And he

---

*See Bacon's Essay *Of Simulation and Dissimulation*, where he will have it that dissimulation is a necessary consequence of " secrecy," its " skirts or traine, as it were." Simulation he holds to be " more culpable . . . except it be in great and rare matters " where there is " no Remedy." Jonson would be able to maintain that his Ode told no lies direct—its attribution of " small Latin " being merely conditional, and its " Swan of Avon " a purely imaginary bird.

knows Heminge and Condell well enough to feel certain that they will not have the smallest objection, either to being assigned prominent places in the forthcoming Book, or to his putting into their mouths statements, etc., concerning Shakespeare, which he himself would shrink from uttering. But even so, the task is no sinecure.

Here guess-work ends.

The famous Folio, with its apparatus of *Dedication*, prefatory *Address*, *Ode*, to " my beloved the author," etc., made its appearance in 1623. The *Dedication* intimates (with ironical emphasis on the word " trifles ") that the author of these " trifles " was dead, " he not having the fate common with some to be exequutor to his owne writings. . . . We have but collected them, and done an office to the dead, to procure his Orphanes, Guardians : without ambition either of selfe-profit, or fame : onely to keepe the memory of so worthy a Friend and Fellow alive, as was our Shakespeare."

The *Address* expresses a wish that the Author had lived to set forth " his owne writings. But since it hath bin ordain'd otherwise, and he by death departed from that right, we pray you do not envie his Friends the office " of collection, etc. This is followed by a statement, probably half jest, half irony, that the Author uttered his thoughts with such " easinesse, that wee have scarse received from him a blot on his papers." That Heminge and Condell had no hand in either *Dedication* or *Address* is sufficiently proved by turns and phrases characteristically Jonsonian. They, I suppose, had given Jonson *carte blanche*, and he made use of the gift, in the interest of literature which might otherwise have suffered irreparable loss. In this way the fiction of Shakespeare's identity with Shakspere was so plausibly documented, that Jonson might have spared himself any further trouble on that score. But either to make assurance doubly sure, or to show his dexterity, he set about the writing of his Ode as if the fiction had not been planted already. Some of the Ode's features need no further comment than they have received. But the " small Latin " and " Swan of Avon " allusions deserve a word or two more. Both passages point at Shakspere and away from Shakespeare. What was their *raison d'être* ? They were exceptionally significant touches to an elaborate system of camouflage, by which posterity, including ourselves, was to be deluded.

Hitherto the accent has been too much on the unessentials of the Ode, and far too little on its beauties. No nobler contemporary appreciation of Shakespeare has reached our ears, and that is a cogent reason for gratitude to its author. Before taking leave of him, I venture to make free with one of his apostrophes. The lines would then run thus :

Soule of the Age !
The applause ! delight ! the wonder of our Stage !
My Bacon rise !

In order to correct misapprehensions which may have arisen through my having slipped into positive statements, where *ex hypothesi* or conditional ones might have been desired, I wish expressly to disclaim any intention to dogmatise. Scientific certainty is out of the question. High probability we may reach, perhaps have reached. But that is the limit. That Bacon was Shakespeare, the only Shakespeare that matters, is merely a working hypothesis. Of other hypothetical Shakespeares who have been put forward, a certain Earl of Rutland would have deserved serious consideration, had he been as able a writer as was his father-in-law, Sidney. The only formidable competing hypothesis might seem to be that of a Great Unknown. But this essentially is a confession of ignorance, and some of its supporters are sceptics who amuse themselves by falling upon every hypothesis in turn.*

* As to Jonson and Shakespeare, see further the extract from an article contributed by Mr. Smithson to *The Nineteenth Century*, prefixed to his Essay on the Masque of *Time Vindicated*. I may be allowed also to refer to my booklet *Ben Jonson and Shakespeare* (Cecil Palmer, 1921).

BACON AND "POESY"

BACON AND "POESY"

BACONIANS hold that Francis Bacon concealed his identity under an *alias*, and this perhaps is why they are sometimes accused of slandering him, as if the use of a pen-name were a crime and not the perfectly legitimate ruse it actually is. Calumniators of Bacon there exist no doubt, and some of them are disposed to give Macaulay as an instance. Such calumniation, however, is less likely to be found among Baconians than among our orthodox opponents, whose creed effectually bars the way to any true appreciation of the great man. As for Mr. William Shakspcrc of Stratford, his character was, or should be, above suspicion. The Burbages, exceptionally well-informed and credible witnesses, testify that he was a " deserving " man, and Baconians accept that valuation of the man all the more readily because there is no proof that he himself ever laid claim to anything published or known as Shakespeare's.

The serious criticism that Baconians have to face may be considered under three heads : (i) The testimony of Ben Jonson ; (ii) The popular notion that Bacon was essentially a man of science ;

(iii) The absence of conspicuous and unmistakable evidence of identity between Bacon and Shakespeare.

(i) In spite of the obvious inconsistency and perversity of Ben Jonson's various utterances, on the subject, and the difficulty of believing that his famous Ode of 1623 could refer except in part to a death which had occurred in 1616, Ben Jonson is commonly regarded as an absolutely conclusive witness against us. An article of mine entitled *Ben Jonson's Pious Fraud*, which appeared in the *Nineteenth Century and After* of November 1913, was an attempt at justification, and the attempt shall not be repeated here. Some of my readers, however, may care to know that in the December (1913) number of the same review an angry opponent charged me with having libelled Ben Jonson, about the last thing of which I, a lifelong admirer of Ben Jonson's, could really be guilty.

(ii) The second criticism we have to meet is founded on the assumption that Science—Natural Science—set her mark upon Bacon almost as soon as he entered his teens. The main business of this section will be to set forth arguments tending to show that the mark which Bacon actually bore from early youth to mature age, was the sign manual of Poetry. In the nineties of the 16th century, Bacon had serious thoughts of abandoning the legal profession into which he had been thrust, and devoting himself to literature in some form or other. Towards the close of his life, when reviewing his life's work, he regretfully confesses to having wronged his " genius " in not devoting himself to letters for which he was " born." In another letter of about the same date, he expresses the same conviction : that in deserting literature for civil affairs, he had done " scant justice " to his " genius." These are not the words, nor this the attitude of a man who thought and felt that he was born for Natural Science. Possibly so, says an opponent, but if Bacon were really born for literature, how came it that his literary output, until he had passed the mature age of 40, was so small ? If you, Baconians, were not blinded by prejudice, you would recognise in Bacon's literary inactivity during youth and early manhood, something very like proof of a preoccupation with Science. In replying to this argument, I should begin by pointing out that the words " literary inactivity " beg the important question of concealment of identity. Waiving this point for the moment, the presumption of an early preoccupation with Science will be seen at a glance to be incompatible with what we know of Bacon's attainments in that direction. A speech of his about 1592 in praise of " Knowledge "—a word which covered everything knowable—contains some of his finest and most characteristic thoughts. The praise of knowledge, he declares, is the praise of mind, since " knowledge is mind. . . . The " minde itself is but an accident to knowledge, for " knowledge is a double of that which is. The " truth of being and the truth of knowing is all " one." Then comes a rhetorical question reminiscent of Lucretius's *suave mari*, i.e.: " Is there " any such happiness as for a man's mind to be " raised above . . . the clowdes of error that turn " into stormes of perturbations . . . Where he

" may have a respect of the order of Nature " ?
" Knowledge," the speaker continues, should enable
us " to produce effects and endow the life of man
" with infinite commodities." At this point he
interrupts himself with the reflection that he " is
" putting the garland on the wrong head," and then
proceeds to inveigh against the " knowledge that is
" now in use : All the philosophie of nature now
" receaved is eyther the philosophie of the Gretians
" or of the Alchemist." Aristotle's admiration of
the changelessness of the heavens is derided on the
naïve assumption that there is a " like invariableness
" in the boweles of the earth, much spiritt in the
" upper part of the earth which cannot be brought
" into masse, and much massie body in the lower
" part of the heavens which cannot be refined into
" spiritt."* Ancient astronomers are next taken
to task for failing to see " how evident it is that
" what they call a contrarie mocion is but an abate-
" ment of mocion. The fixed starres overgoe
" Saturne and Saturne leaveth behind him Jupiter,
" and so in them and the rest all is one mocion,
" and the nearer the earth the slower." As for
modern astronomers, Copernicus for instance, and
Galileo, he dismisses them with contumely as
" new men who drive the earth about." Then he
chides himself for having forgotten that " know-
" ledge itself is more beautiful than any apparel

* In this place the order of the words is slightly altered, but the
quoted words are Bacon's. Here also it may be well to observe that
Francis Bacon was not a pioneer in the revolt against what is called the
Aristotelian, but should be called the Scholastic Philosophy. Destructive
criticism of that philosophy began at least as early as the 13th century
and had already done its work so far as natural science was concerned
long before Francis Bacon took up the cry.

" of wordes that can be put upon it "—a romantic sentiment reminiscent of Biron's " angel knowledge " in *Love's Labour's Lost* ; and a subsequent passage is reminiscent of Montaigne. The conclusion of the Speech is too fine to be abridged and must be given in full :

" But indeede facilitie to beleeve, impatience to " doubte, temeritie to assever, glorie to knowe, end " to gaine, sloth to search, resting in a part of nature, " these and the like have been the things which " have forbidden the happy match between the " minde of man and the nature of things, and in " place thereof have married it to vaine nocions and " blynde experiments. And what the posteritie " of so honorable a match may be it is not hard to " consider.* Therefore no doubte the sovereigntie " of man lieth hid in knowledge, wherein many " things are reserved which Kings with their " treasures cannot buy, nor with their force com- " mand : their spies and intelligencies can give " no news of them : their seamen and discoverers " cannot saile where they grow. Now we governe " nature in opinions but are thrall to her in " necessities, but if we would be led by her in " invention we should command her in action."

These are not the views nor is this the accent of one who has been devoting himself to natural science. The utterance is that of a genius for letters

---

* This always reminds me of *The Tempest* and its projected match between Ferdinand, the unsophisticated mind of man, and Miranda, symbol of the new method of nature study. Naples, the New City of the Tempest, would thus stand for the model city or state expected to spring up as a result of the New Method. The *New Atlantis* of Bacon was another state of this kind.

whose preoccupation has been the apparelling of beautiful thoughts in beautiful words.

The above Speech, which is part of an entertainment called a Conference of Pleasure, expresses intuitions that come from the very soul of the poet-speaker. Ample confirmation of this is to be found in the *Advancement of Learning*—Learning here being the synonym of Knowledge in the Speech—published in 1605. That work aimed at promoting " natural science " with a view above all to scientific discovery and the increase of man's power over nature. It teems with practical allusions to and quotations from the classical poets, particularly Ovid and Vergil. It was dedicated to James the First, a prince—to quote the words of its author—" invested with the learning and universality* of a philosopher." In a passage dealing with the art of medicine the author deems it very much " to the purpose " to note that poets were wont " to " conjoin music and medicine in Apollo, because " the office of medicine is but to tune this curious " harp of man's body and reduce it to harmony." Another passage asserts that the wild fancies of quacks or empirics were anticipated and discredited by the poets in the fable of Ixion. What we call endowment of research, he, student of *belles lettres* that he is, regards as provision for the making of experiments appertaining to Vulcan and Dædalus. Students of Natural Science will search the book in vain for evidence of direct familiarity with any

* In a letter to his uncle, 1592, Bacon wrote : " I have taken all knowledge to be my province." May this explain the " universality " with which James I is here credited ?

branch of the subject. In the opinion of its author, natural history—the natural history of 1605—left little to be desired so far as normal phenomena were concerned. He ruled that the "opinion of Copernicus touching the rotation of the earth" was repugnant to "natural philosophy." The notion that air had or could have weight is dismissed as preposterous. Among his observations on history there is no suggestion of the circulation of the blood. He sums up Gilbert in terms of contempt, his own contribution to the subject of magnetism being : "There is formed in everything "a double nature of good, the one as everything "is a total or substantive in itself, the other as it "is a part or member of a greater or more general "form. Therefore we see the iron in particular "sympathy moveth to the loadstone, but yet if it "exceed a certain quantity, it forsaketh the affection "to the loadstone and like a good patriot moveth "to the earth which is the region or country of "massy bodies."

One of the most telling arguments against the presumption that Bacon had interested himself in natural science to the exclusion of almost everything else, is the staggering value he put upon "poesy" as compared with "philosophy" or science at large. Fascinated by the wonderful discoveries of explorers in the material globe, he pictures knowledge, all knowledge, as an intellectual globe, which he then divides into three great parts or continents, History, Poesy, and Philosophy. Only a poet could have made such a distribution as that. For the continent allotted to Philosophy, as he understands it, embraced not only all the natural sciences, but also ethics, politics, mathematics, metaphysics, and many another subject besides. It would be easy, out of the *Advancement* alone, to multiply refutations of the theory that Bacon's early and middle life were devoted to natural science. The only difficulty is to select.

Before changing the subject it may be well to give the substance of a foot-note to the present writer's *Shakespeare-Bacon*, 1899 (Swan Sonnenschein) : " When Bacon came to review his early " estimate of the importance of poetry to science " or knowledge, he was evidently dissatisfied. In " the *Advancement* (1605) he had claimed that ' for " ' the expressing of affections, passions, corruptions, " ' and customs, we are beholding to poets more " ' than to philosophers.' In the corresponding " place of the revised edition (1623) he drops this " claim. In the *Advancement* again Poesy is stated " to be one of the three ' goodly fields '* (history " and experience being the other two), ' where grow " ' observations concerning the several characters " ' and tempers of men's natures and dispositions.' " In the corresponding place of the revised version this commendation is materially lowered, on the ground that poets are so apt to exceed the truth. The revised version, in short, goes so far towards cheapening Poesy and Imagination as to suggest that if the author had not been hampered by his earlier utterances, he would have deposed both

---

* These same goodly fields had been so diligently cultivated by Bacon that his insight into human nature was probably unequalled by any of his contemporaries, whilst his mastery of all arts of expression enabled him to portray it as it has never been portrayed before or since.

from the high places they still were permitted to occupy in his system.

That Bacon's relations with " Poesy " were extremely intimate and at the same time anxiously concealed from the public, his letters afford convincing evidence. Writing to the Earl of Essex in 1594-5, when his affairs were in evil plight, he assures that generous friend that " the waters of Parnassus " are the best of consolation. In a letter to Lord H. Howard he writes : " We both have tasted of the best waters to knit minds together "—the allusion being of course to the same Parnassian waters. In an open letter (1604) to the Earl of Devonshire, he confesses to having written a sonnet addressed to the Queen herself on a memorable occasion, and then, by way of proving his generosity when the welfare of Essex was at stake, directs special attention to the fact that this sonnet (affair) involved a publishing and declaring of himself—in other words a dropping of the mask that screened him as poet from the eyes of the public. That such was his meaning is explained by a confidential letter to a poetical friend in which he ranks himself among " concealed " poets. Moreover, this was evidently only one of several letters in which Bacon confessed himself a concealed poet, for John Aubrey tells us that Bacon " was a good poet, but concealed as appears by his *letters*." Whether any of these other letters still exist is to be doubted, for the piety of Sir Tobie Mathew, Sir Thomas Meautys, and other devoted friends of the concealed poet, would naturally destroy all they could lay hands on.

BACONIAN ESSAYS

The external evidence that Bacon was essentially a poet is a theme so large that only a portion of it can be given here. In 1626, the year of Bacon's death, John Haviland printed for Sir William Rawley thirty-two *monumenta insignia* expressive of adoration and grief for the great man who had just passed away.* Rawley, the editor, would take care that no published offering to the *Manes Verulamiani* should impart his Master's secret to persons who were not in it already ; and this may help to explain why all the thirty-two offerings are in Latin, not in the vulgar tongue. In his preface to the collection, Rawley informs his readers that the *monumenta* were a selection merely from the numbers which had been entrusted to him—" very many, and those of the very best having been kept back by him " (*plurimos, enim, eosque optimos versus apud me contineo*). How tantalising ! He does not even hint at his reason for such wholesale suppression of masterpieces. One of the thirty mourners declares that Bacon was a Muse more choice than any of the famous Nine. Another considers him " the hinge of the literary world." Another bids the fountain of Hippocrene weep black mud, and warns the Muses that their bay-trees would go out of cultivation now that the laurel-crowned Verulam had left this planet. Others call upon Apollo and the Muses to weep for the loss of the great Bacon. Another laments the disaster that has befallen " us nurselings of the Muses," and calls Bacon " the Apollo of our choir." Another

* " Insignia hæc amoris et mæstitiæ monumenta." These were published by Rawley under the title of *Manes Verulamiani*, in 1626, the year of Bacon's death. [Ed.]

exclaims that " the morning-star of the Muses, the favourite of Apollo, has fallen," and supposes that Melpomene in particular is inconsolable for the loss of him. Another declares that Bacon had placed all the Muses under obligations impossible to estimate. Another laments him as " the Tenth Muse . . . ornament of the choir," and imagines that Apollo can never have been so unhappy before. Another regards Bacon as the *delicium* of his country. Another calls him the choir leader of the Pierides. Another, No. 24, will have it that Ovid, had he lived, would have been better qualified than any other poet to lay an acceptable offering on the tomb of Bacon. Why Ovid should have been pitched upon is not obvious. Perhaps the opinion of Francis Meres, that " the sweet witty soul of Ovid lives in mellifluous and honytongued Shakespeare, witness his *Venus and Adonis*, his *Lucrece*, his *Sugred Sonnets*, among his private friends," may have determined his choice. Here it should be mentioned that a previous contributor had hinted not obscurely at Bacon's authorship of " some elegant love pieces or poems "—*quicquid venerum politiorum.** Another

---

* S. Collins, Rector of King's College, Cambridge, writes, in the *Manes Verulamiani* :

> *Henricus* neque Septimus tacetur,
> Et quicquid venerum politiorum, et
> Si quid præterii inscius libellum
> Quos magni peperit vigor Baconi.

Where the appended translation reads: " Nor must the Seventh Henry fail of mention, or if aught there be of more cultured loves, aught that I unwitting have passed over of the works which the vigor of great Bacon hath produced." A note explains " quicquid venerum politiorum " as " stories of love more spiritually interpreted," and refers to Bacon's *De Sapientia Veterum*.

The author of No. XVIII of the *Manes* tells us that " the Day Star of the Muses hath fallen ere his time ! Fallen, ah me, is the very care and sorrow of the Clarian god [Phœbus to wit], thy darling, nature and the world's—Bacon : aye—passing strange—the grief of very Death.

contributor exclaims : " Couldst thou thyself, O Bacon, suffer death, thou who wert able to confer immortality on the Muses themselves ? " The last of the thirty-two selected contributors is Thomas Randolph, a notable member of the group of wits known as *the tribe of Ben*. After having expatiated on the grief of himself and his fellow-poets for the irreparable loss they had just sustained, and borne his testimony to Bacon's intimacy with the melodious goddesses (Camænæ), Randolph in the manner affected by contemporary poets and men of letters, proceeds to eulogise Bacon as the inventor of new scientific methods, of keys to Nature's labyrinth, etc., and finishes : " But we poets can add nothing to thy fame. Thou thyself art a singer, and therefore singest thine own praises." (*At nostræ tibi nulla ferent encomia musæ, Ipse canis, laudes et canis inde tuas*).

To sum up, the outstanding impression left on the mind by Randolph and his friends is that they regarded Bacon, not merely as a poet, but as the foremost poet of the age ; and this impression is confirmed by the reflection that few if any of the contributors knew enough of science to be capable of appreciating the work of really scientific pioneers such as Harriot, Gilbert, Harvey, and others whose names are onspicuously absent from the roll of Bacon's admirers.

What privilege did not the crule Destiny [*Atropos*, one of the Fates] claim ? Death would fain spare, and yet she [*Atropos*] would not. Melpomene, chiding, would not suffer it, and spake these words to the stern goddesses [the *Parcæ*, or Fates] : ' Never was Atropos truly heartless before now ; keep thou all the world, only give my Phœbus back.' " It is to be noted that the Muse who here speaks of Bacon as her " Phœbus," or Apollo, is Melpomene the Muse of Tragedy. [Ed.]

(iii) The remaining difficulty—that of establishing a relation between Bacon and Shakespeare—has now to be dealt with. It may be well to begin by directing attention to the significant omission of the name of Jonson, head of the *tribe of Ben*, from the collection of eulogies we have just been considering. Adequate explanation of this conspicuous omission is almost impossible without the aid of the Bacon hypothesis. If any contribution of Jonson's had appeared in the publication, the secret would have been out. Even as it was, his executors almost disclosed it when, in 1640-1, they sanctioned publication of those tell-tale notebooks in which Jonson records that Bacon " had performed that in our tongue which might be compared or preferred either to insolent Greece or haughty Rome," an appreciation almost identical with that contained in his famous Ode to Shakespeare. It is well to remember in this connection that Jonson on Bacon's sixtieth birthday had apostrophised him as an enchanter or " mystery " worker.

Among other arguments which tend to identify the names of Bacon and Shakespeare, the following seem worthy of mention : (a) Poesy, as we know, constituted one of the three continents into which Bacon in his *Advancement of Learning*, mapped out the whole " globe " of the knowable. To ignore dramatic poetry altogether would have given rise to inconvenient curiosity. Compelled, therefore, to give it a name, Bacon rejects the natural word "dramatic" and adopts instead the out-of-the-way word " representative." What he says, moreover, about dramatic poetry—in the proper place for saying it—is apparently intended to carry on the suggestion that he was almost a stranger to dramatic performances, a suggestion contradicted by passages in other sections of the same work. For instance, on handling what he calls the " Georgics of the mind," he describes dramatic poetry in terms so appropriate to the best dramatic poetry of the period, that one is almost forced to say to oneself : Here surely, Bacon must have been thinking of Shakespeare ! The passage will bear quoting at length. " In poetry," it runs, " no less than in history, " we may find painted forth with great life how " affections are kindled and excited ; how they " work, how they vary, how they gather and fortify, " how they do fight and encounter one with another " . . . how to set affection against affection, and " to master one by another, even as we use to hunt " beast with beast." His leave-taking, it may be added, of the whole theme or subject of poetry is effected by an ironical : " But it is not good to stay too long in the theatre," which could only be fully appreciated I suppose, by his personal friends.

(b) Nowhere, I believe, in any extant writing of Bacon's, whether letter, essay, or notebook, is there any mention of Shakespeare, and a like reticence is observed in the Rawley collection just cited. Assume for the moment that Shakespeare was the proper name of the man of Stratford, not the pseudonym of Bacon, or, to put it in another way, that Shakespeare and Bacon were two separate persons, and what is the result ? We should have to concede that of two poets, both interested in things dramatic, both supreme judges and keen observers of human nature, its affections, passions, corruptions, and customs—that of two such poets, one, and that one Bacon, must have forbidden the very mention of the other, and this, too, for no discoverable reason.

(c) Bacon (in 1605) held that the chief function of poetry was " to give some shadow of satisfaction to the mind of man in those points wherein the nature of things doth deny it." He ranked poets among the very best of ethical teachers in virtue of their insight into human character as modifiable " by the sex, by the age, by the region, by health and sickness, by beauty and deformity " and the like ; and again . . . " by sovereignty, nobility, obscure birth, riches, want, magistracy, privateness, prosperity, adversity, constant fortune, variable fortune, rising *per saltum*, *per gradus* and the like." Here again many an open-minded reader must have felt moved to reflect that he was on the track, if not in the presence, of Shakespeare.

(d) It is clear that Bacon as he grew older, came to think less and less highly of imaginative work. The mere fact that Shakespeare ultimately abandoned his poetical offspring to chance, points, it surely would seem, to a similar change of view.

(e) Though many of the coincidences between Bacon and Shakespeare may be explained as manifestations of the Time Spirit, some of them strongly suggest direct contact even when taken singly. Take for example, the *misquotation of Aristotle* by Shakespeare in *Troilus and Cressida*, and by Bacon in the *Advancement of Learning*.* Take, again, the curious resemblance between the *Winter's Tale* and the *Essay of Gardens*. Spedding's comment on this passage in the Essay runs: " The scene in *Winter's Tale* where Perdita presents the guests with flowers . . . has some expressions which, if the Essay had been printed somewhat earlier, would have made me suspect that Shakespeare had been reading it."†

(f) Again, certain views to which Bacon gave expression in the *Essay of Deformity*, seem implicit in Shakespeare's *Richard the Third*. Richard has his " revenge of nature " for the ill turn she did him in making him deformed. He is also " extreme bold," ever on the watch to " observe the weakness " of others. His deformity, moreover, must, it would seem, be supposed to have " quenched jealousy " in those personages who, if he had been comely, would have foreseen and thwarted his ambitious designs.

(g) In the course of some interesting observations on the writing of history considered as an art, Bacon confesses to a liking for ready-made outlines or plots, so that the artist might be free to concentrate his powers on the more congenial work of enrichment " with counsels, speeches, and notable particularities." The faulty plots of many of Shakespeare's plays imply that he also grudged

---

* But " moral philosophy," the words used both by " Shakespeare " and Bacon, are the correct translation of τῆς πολιτικῆς. " Political philosophy " would have been a wrong translation. Moreover, Erasmus, before " Shakespeare " and Bacon, had rightly translated πολιτικῆς by " moral philosophy." [Ed.]

† Items (e), (f), (g) and (h) are lifted without material alteration from my *Bacon-Shakespeare* Essay.

the labour of construction and delighted in decoration and enrichment.

(h) Several editions of Bacon's Essays seem to have been published without their author's consent. Shakespeare also seems to have been preyed upon by piratical publishers. Wherever concealment of authorship is a desideratum, prosecution by law must needs be difficult if not impossible.

(i) Whenever Shakespeare, as we know him in quartos and folios, stands in need of an interpreter, no contemporary author is so often consulted by orthodox critics as Francis Bacon.

(k) Compare the *Merchant of Venice*, which the editor of the First Folio rather enigmatically calls *comedy*, with Bacon's *Essay of Usury*. The primary intention of the play was to amuse or delight ; that of the Essay being of course to instruct. But the play appears to me to have combined *utile* with *dulce*, instruction with pleasure ; and the lesson as I understand it was this :—usury instead of being forbidden by the State, should be recognised and regulated, on the ground that unconditional forfeiture of pawns or pledges—the usual alternative to usury—is apt to bear more harshly on the borrower. The crisis of the play arrives near the end of Act IV, Sc. 1, where the Doge pronounces judgment. The instant and immediate effect upon Shylock is positively crushing ; he would rather die than submit. But the accent of despair is quickly succeeded by the words : " I am content," although one of the conditions just introduced by Antonio is that the wretched man Shylock should

" presently become a Christian." The change of mood is so amazing that we can hardly believe our senses. What can be the explanation ? we ask ourselves. Between the judgment pronounced by the Doge and Shylock's accent of despair, Antonio has thrown in these words : " So please my lord the Duke and all the Court to quit the fine for one half of his goods, I am content ; so he [Shylock] will let me have the other half in use, to render it upon his death unto the gentleman that lately stole his daughter." To us the words may seem insignificant. But Shylock was a sort of personification of usury, and to him they meant nothing less than victory—victory over his arch-enemy Antonio, the head and front of the anti-usury party in Venice.

Students of Bacon will remember that his *Essay of Usury* is a plea for State recognition and regulation of interest or " use," on utilitarian grounds similar to those suggested in the comedy.

But may not this harmony between the *Merchant of Venice* and the Essay have been accidental, especially as there was an interval of some twenty-five years between the appearance of the *Essay* in its present form and our *Merchant of Venice* ? My answer is that the *Essay* was based, as we know from one of Bacon's own letters, on " some short papers of mine touching usury, how to grind the teeth of it," etc., and these short papers may well have been written as early as 1598, when Bacon himself was in the clutches of the money-lender.*

---

* The story of the *Merchant of Venice* is, as is well known, founded on the *Pecorone* of Ser Giovanni, Day IV, Novel I. See my *Is there a Shakespeare Problem ?* p 91. *et seq.* [ED.]

BACON AND "POESY"

(l) The relation between the play of *Hamlet* and the *Essay of Revenge* is quite as close as that between the *Essay of Usury* and the *Merchant of Venice*. A reader who should consider the tragedy of *Hamlet* with a single eye to conduct, will hardly escape the reflection that its lesson or moral is summed up to perfection in one of Bacon's Essays, viz., the one which treats of revenge : " They doe but trifle with themselves that labour in past matters. There is no man doth a wrong for the wrong's sake ; but thereby to purchase himselfe Profit, or Pleasure, or Honour, or the like. Therefore why should I be angry with a Man, for loving himselfe better than mee ? . . . Vindicative persons live the Life of Witches : who, as they are Mischievous, so end they Infortunate." Such in the end was the noble Hamlet's fate. Once possessed by the devil of revenge, he becomes a sort of upas or plague-centre, and perishes in a sorry and most unlucky broil.

(m) The existence of striking harmonies between Shakespeare and Bacon was detected by foreign students fifty years ago and more. Professor Kuno Fischer, for example, wrote : " To the parallels between them [i.e. Bacon and Shakespeare] belong the similar relation of both to Antiquity, their affinity to the Roman mind, and their divergence from the Greek. . . . Bacon would have man studied in his individual capacity as a product of nature and history, in every respect determined by . . . external and internal conditions. And exactly in the same spirit has Shakespeare understood man and his destiny." Gervinus in his

BACONIAN ESSAYS

Commentaries observes : " In Bacon's works we find a number of moral sayings and maxims of experience from which the most striking mottoes might be drawn for every Shakespearean play, aye, for all his principal characters, testifying to a remarkable harmony in their comprehension of human nature." One more quotation, of like import and from an author with no partiality for Baconian views, may not be superfluous. Professor J. Nichol, after having ruled out the Baconian heresy by recording his opinion that Bacon did not write Shakespeare, proceeds : " But there is something startling in the like magnificence of speech in which they [Bacon and Shakespeare] find voice for sentiments often as nearly identical when they anticipate as when they contravene the manners of thought and standards of action that prevail in our age." (*Francis Bacon*, Vol. I, 1888).

(n) Only a lawyer by education would have hit upon the technicality which is the nucleus of the 87th Sonnet of Shakespeare. The technicality is not one which an amateur interested in common law proceedings would be likely to pick up, for it belongs to the art of conveyancing. Part of my time, fifty years ago, was spent in the chambers of a conveyancer. But for that early training I might still have been able to see intellectual beauty in the well-known bust of Shakespeare at Stratford ; for my suspicion of the popular legend originated in the conviction that the Shakespeare who matters must have been bred up a lawyer.*

* See also the forty-sixth Sonnet. [Ed.]

BACON AND " POESY "

(o)   In the year 1867, Mr. John Bruce discovered in Northumberland House, which then stood in the Strand, a bundle of Elizabethan manuscripts, the outermost sheet of which contains a miscellaneous list of Elizabethan writings, the majority of which are unquestionably identified with work previously known to have been due to Bacon. The minority consists of five pieces, three of which may, for anything we know to the contrary, have been enriched if not entirely written by him. The two remaining pieces figure in the list as " Rychard the Second " and " Rychard the Third." The significance of this association with work of which there can be no doubt that Bacon was the author, is greatly increased by the fact that the cover or sheet which bears the list of contents is bescribbled at random with the names " ffrancis Bacon " and " William Shakespeare."*

Mr. Spedding evidently missed what seems to me the true significance of this double association— the combination of titles in the list of contents, and the mixture of the names Bacon with Shakespeare in the scribbles. But one or two of his observations on the subject of this singular find are interesting enough. He notes, for example, that the name " Shakespeare " in the scribbles is " spelt in every case as it was always printed in those days, and not as he himself in any known case wrote it." Another of Spedding's observations is that the contained manuscripts, list or lists of contents, and scribbles, all belong to a period " not later then the reign of Elizabeth."

* See my chapter on " The Northumberland Manuscript." *Post* p. 187.

(p) Attentive readers of almost any biography of Francis Bacon will be surprised to learn that the record of his achievements begins so late. Singularly precocious, he has already reached the ripe age— so these biographies tell us—of 36, before anything worthy of mention can be placed to his credit except a small tract or booklet of confessedly unripe *Essays*, *Religious Meditations*, and *Coulers of Good and Evil*. That there must be something very wrong with the record is proved by the fact that already in 1597, the date of the booklet, everything that came, or was suspected of coming, from the pen of Bacon, was in such request that he was compelled, as he tells his brother, to publish these crudities lest they should be stolen or mutilated by piratical printers. His first really notable work, according to the conventional record, is the *Advancement of Learning*, which was not published until two-thirds of his life was behind him. By far the greater part of the remaining third was so absorbed by public affairs, and, after his fall, so harassed by ill-health and private worries, that no literary fruit could have been looked for. Yet its closing years were marked by an unparalleled outburst of literary activity— an outburst which, like the fear of piratical printers expressed in his letter of 1597, means, I take it, that his youth and early manhood had been devoted to the art and practice of literature. Shelley's emphatic assertion that Bacon was a poet leaves the puzzle still unsolved. So, perhaps, does the discovery of harmony after harmony between Bacon and Shakespeare.

But the tension will begin to relax so soon as we

shall have taken time to grasp the significance on these two facts : first, that the dramas attributed to Shakespeare (spelt as it was always printed in those days*) cannot be fitted into the life of the man Shakspere who ended his life, and was evidently content to end it, in what was then a small and rather squalid country town : and second, that the evidence —Ben Jonson's—which is commonly supposed to establish the Stratford case, turns out to be in itself an enigma rather than a solution.

The riddle is almost read when we shall have satisfied ourselves that Bacon was not only a poet but a " concealed " poet, and that by his own confession. And by the time we have been shown Sir T. Mathew's remark, in his letter to Viscount St. Alban : " The most prodigious . . . wit I know . . . is of your Lordship's name though he be known by another," the true and only solution stands revealed.

This letter was written, I imagine, just at the time when the First Folio (of Shakespeare) was the talk of literary London. It was excluded from Sir Tobie Mathew's own *Collection of Letters* (published 1660), but seems to have lived on, in seclusion no doubt, till 1762, by which time all thought about the " concealed poet's " potent art had long been buried with his bones. Basil Montagu gives a copy of it, but Spedding, if I mistake not, ignores it.

This is by no means all the evidence that a better advocate than I could bring to bear on the question in dispute. But no stronger guarantee for the truth

* Not quite " always "—there were some exceptions. [ED.]

of the Bacon hypothesis can be demanded than that it should harmonise a large number of otherwise inexplicable data ; and this demand I hope I may have done something to meet.

For the rival hypothesis, of course, there is much to be said. Never was Golden Bough the child or offspring of an ilex oak. Yet Vergil's beautiful tale for ever adorns the lovely Avernian lake. Stratford-on-Avon was even more to the Shakespeare legend, and thereby may likewise be immortalised. " Doth any man doubt that if there were taken out of men's minds vain opinions, flattering hopes, false valuations, imaginations as one would, and the like, but it would leave the minds of a number of men poor shrunken things, full of melancholy and indisposition and unpleasing to themselves ?"

"THE TEMPEST" AND ITS SYMBOLISM

" THE TEMPEST " AND ITS SYMBOLISM *

The Tempest in the form in which it originally left the author's hand belongs, it would seem, with *A Winter's Tale*, to the period 1607-1610, nearer probably to the 7 than the 10. The ground-plot may well have been adapted, as Herr Dorer suggested, from a story which ultimately got into a Spanish collection of Tales, called *Winter Nights*. Of the actual plot it is not necessary to say much. Twelve years before the opening of the play, Prospero, poet and enchanter, the victim of a wicked cabal, found himself and his daughter, then a mere babe, stranded on a barren island. Fortunately part of his library, consisting of volumes which he prized above everything else in the world, except Miranda, had somehow been allowed to accompany him. In the beloved society of these books and Miranda he managed to pass the time until relief came in the shape of a commotion brought about by his own consummate art.

The true centre of the play, the Sun about which its system revolves, is Miranda. It is for her sake, hers alone, that Prospero displays, and then for ever renounces, an art which he dearly loves and is certain he will miss.

*This Essay was written by Mr. Smithson in the year 1912.

Now there is no evidence fit to be trusted that Shakspere, or, to give him the title he coveted, Mr. William Shakspere of Stratford-upon-Avon, gentleman, was ever a lover of books, none that he ever possessed, or would have cared to possess anything in the shape of a library. Among the various specific bequests of his essentially vulgar Will no such thing as a book is even suggested. About 1613 Shakspere exchanged the mentally stimulating atmosphere of London for the deadly dullness of a mean provincial town. His departure, unwept, unsung, and seemingly not even noticed by any member of the literary world he is supposed to have adorned, may have been demanded by keen personal interest in an enclosure scheme which was then agitating the petty community at Stratford. There is no evidence, no hint even, that it was due to ill-health, and it certainly cannot have been due (as the whole action of Prospero was) to preoccupation with the marriage of a daughter. Daughters he had, it is true, and the younger of them (Judith) married one Thomas Quiney a vintner or tavern-keeper, son of Richard Quiney (an old friend of the Shakspere) who, or whose widow, also kept a tavern. But Judith's marriage took place long after her father's retirement from London must have been resolved on. Shakspere's *highest ambition*—Mr. Sidney Lee tells us—*was to restore among his fellow-townsmen the family repute which his father's misfortunes had imperilled.* This father it seems was a chandler or general dealer, not more illiterate probably than others of the family, who began life in a humble way and afterwards came to grief.

If, as is likely, his debts were inconsiderable, his *ambitious* son should have found little difficulty in restoring the *family repute*, such as it was. The fat-witted lines—*Good friend for Jesus sake forbear, To dig the dust enclosed here*, etc.—which this same son seems to have selected, or composed, or ordered, for his monument, though quite out of keeping with mountains of surmise, are entirely in keeping with all we can properly be said to know of the man. Yet this is the man who is said, on eminent authority, to have conceived and executed *The Tempest*, and what is more to my immediate purpose, to have drawn Prospero in his own image! Belief in this might have been possible, had we known next to nothing about Shakspere or his environment. But the finds of a Halliwell-Phillipps (to take him as a type) have had an effect which the industrious finder certainly did not foresee or intend.

More than thirty years ago the writer came to the double conclusion, (a) that whoever *Shakespeare* might have been, Shakspere was not the man ; (b) that of all the known poets of that day, it was Bacon and Bacon alone who seemed to possess the necessary qualifications. Many of the reasons—none of them beholden to cypher, cryptogram or hocus-pocus of any kind—which made for that conclusion are set forth in a little book, *Bacon-Shakespeare, An Essay* (signed E. W. S., Rome, but published, 1900, in London). Most of the reasons there given have, however, no very definite relation to *The Tempest* and its symbolism.

Shelley saw and asserted that *Bacon was a poet*. But students of Bacon need no Shelley to inform them that Bacon was indeed a poet. His earlier work betrays him. Even the *Advancement of Learning* (1605), tinctured as it is by the pedantic style then coming into fashion, holds just the same truth in solution. To many such students, apology is due for labouring the point. My excuse is the existence of a strong prepossession to the contrary. By what seems to have been an oversight on the part of Bacon, his executors and intimate friends, a letter of his to Sir J. Davies, also a poet, has come down to us, unedited for the public. In this letter Bacon confesses himself a poet, ranks himself in effect amongst *concealed poets*. Aubrey too, thanks probably to a similar oversight, lets us into the same secret that Bacon was a *concealed poet*. Of Bacon's affection for poetry the product (Bacon himself calls it the *work or play*) of the imagination, there is no room for doubt. If other evidence were wanting, the *Sapientia Veterum* (1609) would almost suffice to prove it. As Porphyry's reverence for the elder gods is deducible from his attempt to extract philosophy out of the oracles of antiquity, so Bacon's reverent affection for poetry manifests itself in that elaborate attempt of his to distil philosophy out of what is at bottom a medley of poetical fables. That Bacon, like Prospero, delighted in *poesis* (making) is equally clear. *Poesy*, he says in the *De Augmentis* —*Poesy is a dream of knowledge* (*or* culture), *a thing sweet and varied and that would fain be held partly divine. . . . But now it is time for me to awake* (ut evigilem) *and cleave the liquid ether of philosophy*, etc. This passage, written after 1605, obviously means more than affection for poetry the product.

Only a poet who loved to dream, only a poet for whom the awaking was fraught with pain, however glorious the promise of the dawn, would have written that.

Bacon again, like Prospero, was a lover of books, and happy like him, in the possession of a well-filled library (at Gray's Inn, or Gorhambury, or both). He was an omniverous reader, *tasting* some books (mathematical and astronomical, for example), *swallowing* others, *chewing and digesting a few.* His biographer says of him : *He was a great reader*, but *no plodder upon books.*

About 1607-9, Bacon (in one of his *impetus philosophici*) imagined that at last he really had hit upon an infallible Method of vastly enlarging man's dominion over Nature. The problem was how to launch this Method to the best advantage. Knowing only too well that he would receive no encouragement from living experts in science—the scientists who had arrived as distinguished from those who had not yet started—he fixed his hopes on ingenuous, open-minded Youth. But this is a prosaic way of looking at the matter, and Bacon was a poet. To him the desideratum presented itself as a marriage, a marriage between his *darling philosophy*, as he was wont to call it, and an ideal husband. In the *Redargutio Philosophiarum* men are exhorted to devote themselves to the task of bringing about *a chaste and legitimate wedlock between the mind and nature.* In the *Sapientia Veterum* the same idea appears in a different form : *facultates illas duas Dogmaticam et Empiricam adhuc non bene conjunctas* *et copulatas fuisse.** In the *Delineatio* (c. 1607) he writes : *We trust we have constructed a bride-bed for the marriage of Man's Mind with the Universe.* The same idea (hardly as yet an obsession) makes one of its earliest appearances in a *Speech in Praise of Knowledge*, forming part of a dramatic *jeu d'esprit* entitled *A Conference of Pleasure* (1592). In this *Speech* several things are said to *have forbidden the happy match between the mind of man and the nature of things, and in place thereof have married it to vain notions and blind experiments. And what the issue of so honourable a match may be it is not hard to consider.* With the actual merits of the Method we are but distantly concerned here. What is of importance here is the certainty that Bacon would lose no opportunity of repudiating every suggestion that his beloved child owed anything to the imagination. *It was an usual speech of his lordship's,* says his biographer, *that his Natural History is the world as God made it, and not as men have made it, for it hath nothing of the imagination.*

By this time the inner meaning of *The Tempest*, and also the editorial reason for thrusting it into the leading place of the *First Folio*, may have become apparent. Miranda stands for Bacon's *Darling Philosophy*, and the ingenuous young Ferdinand for the unsophisticated mind of man, the human intellect *cleared and delivered* from *idols*, particularly *idols* of *the theatre*. The issue of so auspicious a match is left, in *The Tempest*, as in the *Conference of Pleasure*, to the imagination. Prospero's cere-

---

* See XXVI *Prometheus, sive status hominis*. [ED.]

monious rejection of his magic robes is an adumbration of Bacon's anxiety to preserve his Philosophy from being calumniated as a poetical dream, a thing *infected with the style of the poets*, as he once (in a fragmentary *Essay of Fame*) confessed himself to be. Devotion to Miranda again is the motive for Prospero's resolve to dismiss Ariel from his service, at a time when Ariel could ill be spared, one feels, by his ageing master. The words *my dainty Ariel I shall miss thee* are eloquent of pain, pain self-inflicted and unexplained, except by a promise wholly uncalled-for by anything that appears on the surface. Ariel on the other hand, tricksy Ariel, incapable of human affection, sick of expecting a long-promised freedom, feels no pain, no regret, nothing but joy at the prospect of slaving it no longer for a despotic master: *Merrily, merrily shall I live now, Under the blossom that hangs on the bough.*

The last words of one of Prospero's closing speeches, *Every third thought shall be my grave*, followed up as they are by the thinly veiled pathos of his appeal in the Epilogue, perplex and distress the reader. *Prospero triumphans*, without one word of warning or explanation, has changed into *Misero supplicans*. Why this sudden revulsion? To my untutored mind it intimates a working-over of the play after Bacon's fall, for the purpose of adapting it, not too obviously, to the altered circumstances of the original author, that *unfortunate* Chancellor who, according to Ben Jonson, *hath filled up all numbers, and performed that in our tongue which may be compared or preferred, either to insolent*

Greece or haughty Rome. The date of this (last) working-over would probably synchronise with the first public or semi-public appearances of the *First Folio* (of *Shakespeare*), of Bacon's *De Augmentis Scientiarum*, and of Ben Jonson's *Time Vindicated*, these four events—with perhaps a Court performance of the adapted *Tempest* thrown in—being, I venture to think, intimately connected with what may be called an Apotheosis of Bacon.

" A remarkable story indeed "—an objector may say—" but do you seriously believe that Bacon can be proved to have been the Author, and *Shakespeare* the pen-name ? Besides, does it really matter—except to Stratford and Verulam—whether *Shakespeare* hailed from this place or that ? We have the poems and we have the plays, and that is enough. As for your reading of *The Tempest*, it may be ingenious, but it is not convincing. Patience, with a modicum of ingenuity, has probably never despaired of cajoling almost any given meaning out of any fable—fables, like dreams and Delphian utterances, being almost as plastic as wax. Moreover, the inner meaning you claim to have disclosed, involves the absurdity of supposing that a fable was invented for the express purpose of wrapping up the said meaning, so effectually as to ensure its being missed by all the world, a few esoteric contemporaries only excepted. The idea, to be quite candid, belongs rather to Bedlam than to Bacon."

Strict proof, I reply, is hardly to be expected either now or hereafter. A high degree of probability, resting on evidence of various kinds and different degrees of cogency, is all that the writer has ever contended for. The history of literature abounds in instances of pseudonymity. Of these one of the most apposite that occurs to me is that of Aristophanes, who made use of the name Callistratus, a contemporary actor, to mask his (own) authorship of the *Birds*, *Lysistrata*, etc. There are differences, of course, between the two cases, one being that in that of Aristophanes there were no very obvious reasons for concealment, whereas in the case of Bacon there were several. Whether it really matters who the great poet was depends on the word " really." It certainly does not matter in the sense in which the high price of coal, the low price of Consols, England's relations with other Powers, etc., matter. It does matter for *The Tempest*, the symbolism of which probably extends beyond Miranda and Prospero, as far as Neapolis, and possibly further. It cannot fail to affect the interpretation of other plays of *Shakespeare*. It solves, or helps to solve, interesting problems in the life and acknowledged works of Bacon. It matters in short for all genuine admirers of English literature. As to plasticity—where the fable to be juggled is vague, undocumented, variously and incoherently documented, or frugal of features, the operation will be child's play. With such a fable as *The Tempest* the trick can only be brought off by singling out one or two features and shutting the eye to all the rest. One objection only remains to be dealt with. The reference to Bedlam with which it concludes might have been omitted, but no discussion of this question seems quite in order without some innuendo that the unorthodox person is mad or a crank. The objection itself (though the phrasing might be challenged as favouring the objector) is pertinent enough, and may be answered as follows : Bacon was an inveterate treasure-seeker. The unsunned treasures he sought were not material things like gold and silver, but gems of thought hidden away in the dreamlands of poetry. The genesis of this habit was no doubt closely related to his theory that poesy enables the artist in words to *retire* and *obscure* . . . *secrets and mysteries* by *involving* them in *fables* invented for the purpose, a practice by no means uncommon, he firmly believed, among the poets of antiquity when they wished to reserve information for *selected auditors*.

So far the discussion has been grave to the point of dullness. Would that I had been able to enliven it, if only because *The Tempest* is a comedy—heads the file of the comedies in the *First Folio*. Possibly the following quotation from the work of an eminent critic may help to remedy the fault: *Miranda . . . and her fellow Perdita are idealizations of the sweet country maidens whom Shakspere* (sic) *would see about him in his renewed family life at Stratford.**

---

* It is a pity that Mr. Smithson has not given us the reference to this delightfully comic, but highly characteristic utterance. [ED.]

THE COMMON KNOWLEDGE OF SHAKESPEARE AND BACON

THE COMMON KNOWLEDGE OF SHAKESPEARE AND BACON

MANY years ago, when, not having bestowed a thought upon the subject, I was, naturally, of the orthodox Stratfordian faith, and knew nothing of the Baconian " heresy " except the time-honoured joke that " Shakespeare " was not written by Shakespeare, but by another gentleman of the same name (which I thought " devilish funny ") I happened to be reading Bacon's *Essay on Gardens*. This passage at once arrested my attention : " In April follow, the double violet ; the wall-flower ; the stock-gilliflower ; the cowslip ; *flower-de-luces, and lillies of all natures.*" Why, thought I, those last words are almost identical with some used by Perdita at the conclusion of her lovely catalogue of flowers ! I turned to the *Winter's Tale* (IV. 4) and there read :

> lillies of all kinds,
> The flower-de-luce being one.

For at least half a minute I thought, in my innocence, that I had made a discovery ! But reflection of course, told me that so startling a parallelism must have been observed by hundreds before me. " Lillies of all kinds," says Shakespeare ;

" lillies of all natures," says Bacon ; and each specifies " the flower-de-luce " as one of them ! Surely, I said to myself, this is no mere coincidence ! Surely one of these writers must have, consciously or unconsciously, taken the words from the other ! On closer inspection, too, I found a remarkable resemblance between the two lists of flowers, Bacon's and Shakespeare's ; that they are in fact substantially the same. Did then Shakspere borrow from Bacon ? Very possibly, I thought ; but on investigation I found that the *Essay on Gardens* was first printed in 1625, nine years after player Shakspere's death. Well, then, did Bacon borrow from Shakspere in this instance ? Few, I think, would be inclined to adopt that hypothesis. The author of the *Essay* had made a life-long study of gardens, and, as Mr. James Spedding writes (though I did not discover this till years afterwards), " it is not probable that Bacon would have anything to learn of William Shakespeare [i.e., Shakspere of Stratford] concerning the science of gardening." " Moreover," says the same writer, " the scene in *Winter's Tale* where Perdita presents the guests with flowers . . . has some expressions which, if the *Essay* had been printed somewhat earlier, would have made me suspect that Shakespeare had been reading it ! "* Yes, indeed, and these " expressions," almost identical in both, have made some persons " suspect " that the same pen wrote both the *Essay* and the *Scene*.

There are, as all those who have studied the two authors are aware, many other striking coincidences

* *Bacon's Works*, edited by Spedding, vi, 486.

to be found in the writings of Shakespeare and Bacon. In this chapter I propose to consider some of them only, namely those which, nearly twenty years ago, formed the subject of a controversy between the late Judge Webb, and the late Professor Dowden.

In the year 1902 the late Judge Webb, then Regius Professor of Laws, and Public Orator in the University of Dublin, published a book which he called *The Mystery of William Shakespeare*. The eighth chapter of that work treats " Of Shakespeare as a Man of Science," and here the learned Judge put forward a number of parallelisms taken from Shakespeare's plays and Bacon's works (mainly from the *Natural History*, which was published eleven years after the death of Shakspere of Stratford), in order to show that " the scientific opinions of Shakespeare so completely coincide with those of Bacon that we must regard the two philosophers as one in their philosophy, however reluctant we may be to recognize them as actually one."

To this the late Professor Dowden replied, in *The National Review* of July, 1902, and brought forward an immense amount of learning to show that these coincidences really prove nothing, because " all which Dr. Webb regards as proper to Shakespeare and Bacon was, in fact, *the common knowledge or common error of the time*." Whereunto the Judge, in a brief rejoinder (*National Review*, August, 1902), intimated that all he was concerned with was " the common knowledge and common error of Shakespeare and Bacon," his case being that in matters of science these two, as a fact, show an extremely close agreement. The question for the reader, therefore, is whether or not that agreement is so remarkable that something more than " the common knowledge or common error *of the time* " is required to explain it.

Here the matter has been left, but I think it may be of interest to consider once more the points at issue between these two learned disputants. Let me premise that I do not write as a " Baconian." The hypothesis that Bacon was the author of the plays of Shakespeare, or some of them, or some parts of them, may be mere " madhouse chatter," as Sir Sidney Lee has styled it, or we may be content with more moderate language, and merely say that the hypothesis is " not proven." I leave that *vexata quæstio* on one side. But, whatever may be our opinion with regard to it, it must, I think, be admitted that some of the " parallelisms," or " coincidences," between Bacon and Shakespeare are really very remarkable, and the controversy between Judge Webb and Professor Dowden, which I here pass under review, has not, as it seems to me, so conclusively explained their existence as to leave nothing further for the consideration of an impartial critic.

Let me take an example. Bacon in his *Sylva Sylvarum*, or *Natural History** (Cent. I, p. 98), speaks of " the spirits or pneumaticals that are in all tangible bodies," and which, he says, " are scarce known." They are not, he tells us, as some suppose, virtues and qualities of the tangible parts

* First published in 1627, a year after Bacon's death.

which " men see," but " they are things by themselves," i.e., entities.   And again (Cent. VII, 601),
he says, " all bodies have spirits, and pneumatical
parts within them," and he goes on to point out the
differences between the " spirits " in animate, and
those in inanimate things.   Further on (Cent. VII,
693), Bacon writes : " It hath been observed by the
ancients that much use of Venus doth dim the
sight," and the cause of this, he says, " is the expense
of spirits."   Now in Sonnet 129 Shakespeare
writes :

> The expense of spirit in a waste of shame
> Is lust in action.

Here we certainly seem to have a remarkable
agreement between Shakespeare and Bacon. Both
use the very same expression " the expense of
spirit " and (which constitutes the real strength
of the parallel) both use it in exactly the same
application. What is Professor Dowden's explanation ? He says that " the mediæval theory
of ' spirits ' will be found in the *Encyclopædia of
Bartholomew Anglicus on the Properties of Things*,"
which he says was " a book of wide influence."
He says further : " The popular opinions of
Shakespeare's time respecting ' spirits ' may be
read in *Bright's Treatise of Melancholy*, 1586, and
Burton's Anatomy, 1621, and in many another
volume. . . . Bright, in his *Melancholy*, seems
almost to anticipate the theory of Bacon, and
possibly he was himself influenced by Paracelsus."
As to the expression " expense of spirit," he says
it may be found in this book of Bright's (pp. 62, 237,

and 244), and in Donne's *Progress of the Soul*. I do not understand the Professor to suggest that the Stratford player had consulted these works (Burton, of course, is out of the question) for he writes: "The language of Shakespeare is popular, and connected probably neither with what Bright nor what Bacon wrote, but if a theory be required, it can be found as easily in a volume which Shakespeare might have read, as in a volume published after his death." Bacon, however, we may say with confidence, knew these books, and had, in all probability, read them. The Professor, for instance, refers to Paracelsus, and subsequently, on another point, to Scaliger. Bacon, as we know, was familiar with both these writers, and makes reference to them (see, for instance, *Natural History*, Cent. IV, 354, and Cent. VII, 694), whereas it will, I suppose, hardly be suggested that the player had sought inspiration in the works of these scholars.

The first question, then, which suggests itself is this. Are we to conclude, because there is a theory of " spirits " (which Bacon says " are scarce known") to be found in Bartholomew Anglicus, and Bright, and Paracelsus, that it was a matter of " popular " knowledge, a subject with which Shakspere of Stratford, as well as the philosopher of Gorhambury, would have been likely to be familiar ? This question seems to me a very doubtful one, but if it is to be answered in the affirmative, then we have to ask : Is this assumed popular knowledge, or popular error, sufficient to account for the use by both Shakespeare and Bacon of exactly the same expression in exactly the same collocation ? And in considering this question we must remember that the evidence is cumulative, i.e., this coincidence is not a solitary instance, but only one of many, and it is but fair, if we wish to come to a just decision, that all of them should be considered together.

But how far is it true, as Professor Dowden alleges. it to be, that " Bright in his *Melancholy* seems almost to anticipate the theory of Bacon ? " The book is a scarce one. There is no copy in the London Library. However I have taken the trouble to examine it at the British Museum. Professor Dowden refers to pages 62, 237, and 244. In the edition which I examined, that of 1586, there is no reference to the " expense of spirits " at p. 237. Neither is there at p. 62. On page 63, however, I find the following. The author, one Timothy Bright, " Doctor of Phisicke," is speaking of strong affections of the mind, and he says: " If it holde on long and release not, the nourishme nt will also faile, the increase of the body diminish, and the flower of beautie fade, and finally death take his fatall hold ; which commeth to passe, not onely by *expence of spirit*, but by leaving destitute the parts, whereby declining to decay, they become at length unmeete for the entertainment of so noble an inhabitant as the soule," etc. On p. 244 we read: " Now as all contention of the mind is to be intermitted, so especially that whereto the melancholicke person most hath given himself before the passion is chiefly to be eschued, for the recoverie of former estate and restoring the depraved conceit and fearefull affection. For there, if the affection of liking go withal, both hart and braine do over prodigally *spend their spirite* and with them the subtilest parts of the naturall iuyce [juice] and humours of the bodie. If of mislike and the thing be by forcible constraint layd on, the distracting of the mind, from the promptness of affection, breedeth such an agonie in our nature that thereon riseth also great *expence of spirit*, and of the most rare and subtile humours of our bodies, which are as it were the seate of our naturall heate," etc.

Now in both these passages we find, indeed, the expression the " expense of spirit," but, except for that, it appears that they can hardly be cited as parallel passages with those of either Bacon or Shakespeare. It is not alleged that this expression is peculiar to these two writers—assuming the duality. The parallelism consists in this, that they both use the words in connection with what Bacon terms " the use of Venus." I cannot see that the passages in Bright's treatise, when they are carefully examined, make this parallelism at all less remarkable.

The Professor further tells us that the expression " expense of spirits " may be found in Donne's *Progress of the Soul** Stanza VI. I do not find it in that stanza, but in Stanza V the following occurs. The poet prays that he may be free,

From the lets
Of steep ambition, sleepy poverty,
Spirit-quenching sickness, dull captivity,
Distracting business, and from beauty's nets,
And all that calls from this, and t' others whets,
O let me not launch out, but let me save
Th' expence of brain, and spirit, that my grave
His right and due, a whole unwasted man, may have.

* This work seems to have been first published in 1612.

And in Stanza XXI are the words quoted by Professor Dowden, concerning the sparrow :

> Freely on his she friends
> He blood, and spirit, pith and marrow spends.

This indeed proves, what nobody has ever denied, viz., that the expression " to spend the spirit " is not confined among writers of the Elizabethan age to Bacon and Shakespeare. To what extent it detracts from the force of the coincidence on which Judge Webb has laid stress, I must leave it to the reader to determine. The learned Judge laughs at the idea that citations from Bright's *Treatise of Melancholy* and Donne's *Progress of the Soul*, are proof that the expression was one in common use.

There is another example of agreement between Bacon and Shakespeare in connection with this theory of " spirits." Jessica says (*Merchant of Venice*, V. 1) :

> I am never merry when I heare swet music.

To which Lorenzo replies :

> The reason is your spirits are attentive.

Bacon writes (*Natural Hist.* Cent. VIII, 745) : " Some noises help sleep ; as the blowing of the wind, the trickling of water, humming of bees, *soft singing*, reading, etc. The cause is for that *they move in the spirits a gentle attention.*"

Upon this Professor Dowden tells us that Bright talks of music " alluring the spirites," while " Burton quotes from Lemnius, who declares that music not only affects the ears, ' but the very arteries, the vital and animal spirits,' and, again from Scaliger, who explains its power as due to the fact that it plays upon ' the spirits about the heart,' whereupon Burton, like Shakespeare's Lorenzo, proceeds to speak of the influence of music upon beasts, and like Lorenzo, cites the tale of Orpheus." But Burton's *Anatomy* was not published till 1621, about five years after Shakspere's death, and we can hardly suppose that the player delved into " Lemnius " or " Scaliger ! " But we shall doubt- less be told that, whether Shakspere had read these books or not, the fact that Bright speaks of music alluring the spirits shows that this was a common expression, and that Lorenzo's words are to be referred to " the common knowledge or the common error of the time." But Lorenzo says, " your spirits are *attentive*," and Bacon speaks of " a gentle *attention* " of the spirits. I do not see this expression in Bright, or Lemnius, or Scaliger, as quoted by Professor Dowden. Here, then, we have two expressions, " the expense of spirits " in connection with Venus, and " the attention of spirits " in connection with music, both in Shake- speare and Bacon. It will be for every reader who is interested in the question, taking these coin- cidences with many others of a similar character, to decide whether " the common knowledge of the time " affords a sufficient explanation. And let him remember two things—first, that it is, of course, impossible to find an agreement between Shakespeare and Bacon on a subject of which they two alone (if two they were) had exclusive know- ledge, and secondly that though one, or two, or three threads may not suffice to bear a weight, a great many threads combined into a cord may do so. At any rate, it may be said of these two :

> Utrumque vestrum incredibili modo
> Consentit astrum.

Judge Webb, of course, refers to the well-known fact that both Shakespeare and Bacon held similar views on the relationship of Art to nature, both holding that art was not something different from nature, but a part of nature.   All will remember the dialogue between Perdita and Polixenes in the *Winter's Tale* :

> *Per. :* . . . The fairest flowers o' the season
> Are our carnations and streak'd gillyvors,
> Which some call nature's bastards ; of that kind
> Our rustic garden's barren : and I care not
> To get slips of them.

> *Pol. :* . . . Wherefore, gentle maiden,
> Do you neglect them ?

> *Per. :* . . . For I have heard it said
> There is an art which in their piedness shares
> With great creating nature.

> *Pol. :* . . . Say there be ;
> Yet nature is made better by no mean,
> But nature makes that mean : so, over that art
> Which you say adds to nature, is an art
> That nature makes. You see, sweet maid, we marry
> A gentler scion to the wildest stock
> And make conceive a bark of baser kind
> By bud of nobler race : this is an art
> Which does mend nature, change it rather, but
> The art itself is nature.

It certainly seems remarkable that the King of Bohemia should lecture the country girl on the essential identity of nature and art. It is not exactly what we should have expected. It is somewhat strange, too, to find Bacon waxing eloquent on the same subject, and to the same effect. Take the following from the *De Augmentis* (Lib. II, Cap. ii.): " Libenter autem historiam artium, ut historiæ naturalis speciem, constituimus : quia inveteravit prorsus opinio, *ac si aliud quippiam esset ars a natura, artificialia a naturalibus.* . . . Sed et illabitur etiam animis hominum aliud subtilius malum ; nempe, *ut ars censeatur solummodo tanquam additamentum quoddam, naturæ,* cujus scilicet ea sit vis, ut naturam, sane, vel inchoatam perficere, vel in deterius vergentem emendare, vel impeditam liberare ; minime vero penitus vertere, transmutare, aut in imis concutere possit : quod ipsum rebus humanis præproperam desperationem intulit."

That is to say, " we very willingly treat the history of art as a form of natural history ; for an opinion has long been prevalent *that art is something different from nature*—things artificial from things natural. . . . There is likewise another and more subtle error which has crept into the human mind, namely, that of considering art as merely an assistant* to nature, having the power indeed to finish what nature has begun, to correct her when lapsing into error, or to set her free when in bondage, but by no means to change, transmute, or fundamentally alter nature. And this has bred a premature despair in human enterprises." He goes on to point out that, on the contrary, there is no essential difference between art and nature,

---

* *Additamentum*, an addition, or accession to.

things artificial being simply things natural as affected by human agency, which is a part of nature, so that in the words of Shakespeare, " the art itself is nature."[*]

Here it may be worth while to point out that these words are not to be found in the English *Advancement of Learning*, first printed in 1605, but are found in the enlarged Latin version made under Bacon's supervision, and published in 1623, the very year in which the *Winter's Tale* also first saw the light in print, to wit in the *First Folio*. The play may, no doubt, have been written some ten years before that, but whether in its earlier form it contained all this not very appropriate philosophy concerning art and nature, it is of course impossible to say. It is said to have been written about 1611, and we find Bacon writing about the same time very much to the same effect as above quoted.[†]

Artificial selection is, therefore, after all only a form and part of natural selection, the *differentia* being that it is human agency which brings it into play. And that Bacon had, by one of his luminous intuitions, which are really quite as remarkable as

[*] At contra, illud animis hominum penitus insidere debuerats artificialia a naturalibus, non forma aut essentia, sed efficiente solummodo differre ; homini quippe in naturam nullius rei potestatem esse, præter-quam motus, ut scilicet corpora naturalia aut admoveat, aut amoveat. . . Itaque natura omnia regit : subordinantur autem illa tria ; cursu, naturæ ; exspatiatio naturæ ; et ars, sive additus rebus homo.

[†] " It is the fashion to talk as if art were something different from nature, or a sort of addition to nature, with power to finish what nature has begun, or correct her when going aside. In truth, man has no power over nature except that of motion—the power, I say, of putting natural bodies together, or separating them—the rest is done by nature within." *Descriptio Globi Intellectualis*, circ. 1612. Man (e.g) as the modern writer puts it, " can bring together the radium and the bouillon, but the radiobe, whatever it may be, is none the less a product of nature." " The art itself is nature."

his inductive philosophy, a foreshadowing of the theory of evolution is undeniable, for we have it plainly stated in his *Natural History* (Cent. VI, 525) : " This work of the transmutation of plants one into another is *inter magnalia naturæ* ; for the *transmutation of species* is, in vulgar philosophy, pronounced impossible, and certainly it is a thing of difficulty, and requireth deep search into nature ; but seeing there appear some manifest instances of it, the opinion of impossibility is to be rejected, and the means thereof to be found out."*

As to the " streaked gillivors, which some call nature's bastards," we find that Bacon has much to say concerning experiments in the colouration and variation of these gillyflowers. In the *Natural History* (Cent. VI, 506), he writes : " Amongst curiosities I shall place coloration, though it be somewhat better : for beauty in flowers is their pre-eminence. It is observed by some that gilly-flowers . . . that are coloured, if they be neglected, and neither watered, nor new molded, nor transplanted, will turn white." Subsequently (510) we read : " Take gillyflower seed, of one kind of gillyflower, as of the clove gillyflower, which is the most common, and sow it, and there will come up gillyflowers some of one colour and some of another," etc. Then, in 513, we come to the application of " art " to these flowers : " It is a curiosity also to make flowers double, which is

---

* Unfortunately, however, Bacon's instances are far from satisfactory. " We see," he says, " that in living creatures, that come of putrefaction, there is much transmutation of one into another ; as caterpillars turn into flies, etc. And it should seem probable, that whatsoever creature, having life, is generated without seed, that creature will change out of one species into another." And so forth.

effected by often removing them into new earth. . . .
Inquire also whether *inoculating* of flowers, as stock-
gillyflowers . . . doth not make them double."

At any rate it must, I think, be admitted that we
have here some very remarkable resemblances
between Bacon and Shakespeare. First we have,
as mentioned in the opening of this chapter, an
almost complete verbal agreement, " lillies of all
kinds, the flower-de-luce being one," and " flower-
de-luces and lillies of all natures " ; then we have
two very similar lists of flowers according to the
seasons, whether of the year, or of human life ;
then we have a complete and, I think extraordinary
agreement, as to the philosophy of " nature " and
" art "—to wit, that the two are essentially one,
since art is but part of nature. Moreover it seems
that both writers, if two there were, were writing
these things just about the same time. And
finally we find that both writers are much concerned
with the colours and varieties of " streaked gilly-
vors " or " stock-gillyvors."*

What does Professor Dowden say to this ? He
quotes William Harrison's *Description of England* :
" How art also helpeth nature in the dailie colour-
ing, dubling, and enlarging the proportion of our
floures, it is incredible, to report," etc. But Harrison
does not say, as Shakespeare and Bacon say, that the
art is part of nature (" The art itself is nature ").
He merely speaks of art as an *additamentum quoddam*

* Judge Webb does not refer to Bacon's remarks on the coloration
of flowers which I have thought worth citing, but he quotes the *Natural
History* to the effect that " if you can get a scion to grow upon a stock
of another kind " it " may make the fruit greater, though it is like it
will make the fruit baser." But this is not much of a " parallel " with
the remark of Polixenes as to marrying " a gentler scion to the wildest
stock," etc.

naturæ, which is just the proposition that Bacon (and Shakespeare, by implication) condemns as fallacious. Professor Dowden then tells us that this thought as to art and nature was prominent in the teaching of Paracelsus whom Bacon refuses to honour. But whether or not Bacon refuses to honour Paracelsus he was, at any rate, familiar with him, and makes frequent mention of him. So again as to Pliny, whom the Professor appeals to in this matter. Bacon cites him in the very passage of the *De Augmentis* (Lib. II, Cap. ii), part of which I have quoted. It seems rather remarkable that the authors to whom the Professor makes his appeal should be, so frequently, writers such as Pliny, and Paracelsus, and Scaliger who certainly were well known to Bacon. I doubt if the Stratford player had included these in his (assumed) omnivorous reading ; nor do I think " the common knowledge and common error of the time " explain these coincidences of thought and expression in an altogether satisfactory way. The lines,

this is an art
Which does mend nature, change it rather, but
The art itself is nature,

really do seem to bear the Baconian stamp on the face of them. However those who think it sufficient to find that something similar (though certainly not the same) was said by somebody else somewhere about the same time will doubtless be satisfied with Professor Dowden's hypothesis of a common origin in common knowledge, or error ; and those who are " convinced against their will," will, as usual, be " of the same opinion still." They should note, however, that Mr. Spedding candidly admits that if the *Essay on Gardens* had been published before 1616, he would have suspected that it had been read by Shakespeare !

It is interesting to note that Shakespeare speaks of plants as distinguished by sex difference. An old friend of mine, now, alas, gone to that bourne whence no traveller returns, who, like many others, used to maintain that " everything can be found in Shakespeare " (a proposition which if confined within reasonable limits I should be the last to dispute) was so struck by this fact that, in an article contributed by him to the *Saturday Review*, he expressed the opinion that " it can only be explained as a flash of genius hitting on an obscure truth by a great observer, as Shakespeare undoubtedly was." And in a note to this article, when published with others in book form, he says : "I claim the discovery in the case of flowers for Shakespeare."* But the conception of sex-difference in plants originated long before the days of Shakespeare. It is, if I remember rightly, to be found in Herodotus. But however that may be, it was certainly well known to Bacon who writes (*Nat. Hist.* Cent. VII, 608) : " For the difference of sexes in plants they are oftentimes by name distinguished, as male-piony, female-piony, male-rosemary, female-rosemary ; he-holly, she-holly," etc. He goes on to notice the case of the he-palm and the she-palm, which were said to fall violently in love with one another, as to which further details may be found in Burton's *Anatomy of Melancholy*. Bacon adds : " I am apt

---

* *Country Matters in Short*, by W. F. Collier, p. 21.

enough to think that this same *binarium* of a stronger and a weaker, like unto masculine and feminine, doth hold in all living bodies."*

To return for a moment to Professor Dowden. I should be the last to deny that he states the case against Judge Webb, so far as regards these Shakespeare-Bacon parallelisms, with great force and learning, and what in an "orthodox" critic is, perhaps, best of all, with admirable temper. And in some cases, I am free to admit that he seems to me to have the best of the argument.

But let us take another example. Hamlet, in his letter to Ophelia, writes :

> Doubt thou the stars are fire,
> Doubt that the sun doth move ;
> Doubt truth to be a liar ;
> But never doubt I love.

Upon this Judge Webb comments that Bacon, notwithstanding the teaching of Bruno, and of Galileo, maintained that " the celestial bodies, most of them, are fires or flames as the Stoics held," and that, notwithstanding the teaching of Copernicus, he held the mediæval doctrine of " the heavens turning about in a most rapid motion." And he adds, with a touch of sarcasm : " The marvel is that the omniscient Shakespeare with his superhuman genius maintained these exploded errors as confidently as Bacon." Whereunto Professor Dowden replies that " it presses rather hardly

---

* See also his remarks on the saying " homo est planta inversa," Cent. VII, 607, and compare Burton, *Anat : of Melancholy*, vol. 2, p. 193. Ed. 1800. The scientific facts with regard to sex-difference in the vegetable world were not discovered till some seventy years after Shakspere's death.

upon Hamlet's distracted letter to deduce from his rhyme ' a theory of the celestial bodies,' " and he goes on to say that, " in fact Shakespeare repeats the reference to the stars as fires many times," and that " references to the stars as fire and to the motion of the heavens are scattered over the pages of Shakespeare's contemporaries as thickly as the stars themselves."

Now all this about the stars might, as it seems to me, have been omitted altogether. To assert that the fixed stars are " fire " is surely not to be taken as a proof of scientific ignorance ! The sun itself is but a star, and all of us have read of the " mighty flames," as Sir Robert Ball calls them, that leap from the surface of the sun.* But to affirm " that the sun doth move " as one of the certainties of human knowledge was in Shakespeare's time tantamount to a rejection of the heliocentric teaching of Copernicus and Bruno in favour of the old Ptolemaic system, or, at any rate, of a system in which the earth is supposed to be at rest.† Now, that Bacon had failed to profit by the teaching of Copernicus is certain, for in his *Descriptio Globi Intellectualis* and *Thema Cœli* (1612) he condemns all the then existing systems of Astronomy as

---

* At the same time we must take note, that Bacon's theory of the flamy substance of which the stars are supposed to consist, seems to differ not a little from the modern conception of matter in a state of combustion or incandescence. See Abbott's *Life of Bacon*, pp. 374-5.

† Sir Edward Sullivan, who appears to have been captivated by Signor Paolo Orano's quite untenable theory that Hamlet is meant for Giordano-Bruno, makes a truly remarkable comment upon the second of the lines above-quoted, viz. : " Doubt that the sun doth move." He says this line " is the Copernican System in little " ! It is, of course, the very opposite. *It is the Ptolemaic System in little* ! (See Sir E. Sullivan in *The Nineteenth Century*, February, 1918).

unsatisfactory. His biographer, Dr. Abbott, who is very far from being an indulgent critic, finds much excuse for him here in the fact that Copernicus " himself advocated his own system merely as an hypothesis," and that it was inconsistent and incomplete until Newton had discovered the Law of Gravitation. He adds : " It is creditable to Bacon's faith in the uniformity of nature, that he predicted that future discoveries would rest ' upon observation of the common passions and desires of matter '—an anticipation of Newton's law of attraction."*

But granting that Bacon and Shakespeare were at one in their rejection of the teaching of Copernicus, Bruno, and Galileo, it seems to me that no argument on behalf of the Baconian theory can be safely founded upon that fact. For the " Stratfordian " answer is very simple, viz., that William Shakspere, the Stratford player and supposed author, very naturally was not abreast of the most advanced scientific teaching of his day. He, of course, conceived that the sun moved round the earth as Ptolemy taught, and not *vice versâ*. The argument therefore can only be effective (if at all) as against those Shakespeariolaters who conceive that player Shakspere was omniscient, or, at least, wrote, as it were, by plenary inspiration.

Mr. Edwin Reed, however, makes another use of these lines. He points out that in the Quarto

---

* *Life*, pp. 373-4. Mill remarks (*Logic*, vol. i, p. 253) that Newton's discovery " is the greatest example which has yet occurred of the transformation, at one stroke, of a science which was still to a great degree merely experimental into a deductive science."

of 1603 they do not run as above quoted, but as follows :

> Doubt that in earth is fire,
>   Doubt that the stars do move,
> Doubt truth to be a liar,
>   But do not doubt I love,

and he refers to Bacon's *Cogitationes de Natura Rerum*, assigned to the latter part of 1603, or the early part of 1604, and quotes a passage from his *De Principiis atque Originibus*, in order to show that at that date Bacon had changed his mind in regard to the commonly accepted belief in the existence of a mass of molten matter at the centre of the earth, and maintained that, on the contrary, the terrestrial globe is cold to the core. He goes on to suggest that the substitution of " the sun " for " the stars," giving us the line,

> Doubt that the sun doth move,

in the 1604 edition, is indicative of a deliberate intention on the part of the writer to retain " the doctrine that the earth is the centre of the universe around which the sun and stars daily revolve." So that, in spite of Copernicus, and Bruno, and Kepler and Galileo, Bacon and the author of the Plays " were agreed in holding to the cycles and epicycles of Ptolemy, after all the rest of the scientific world had rejected them, and they were also agreed in rejecting the Copernican theory after all the rest of the scientific world had accepted it." And the same doctrine is, of course, retained in the Folio edition of *Hamlet*, published in 1623, in which same year Bacon wrote, in the third book of the

De Augmentis, that the theory of the earth's motion is absolutely false !

All this is ingenious, but how far it is convincing must be left for the reader's consideration.

Let us take yet another example. Bacon in his *Natural History* (s. 464) tells us that " as terebration doth meliorate fruit, so upon the like reason doth letting of plants blood," the difference being that the blood-letting is only to be effected " at some seasons " of the year. And so also the gardener in Richard II says :

> We at time of year
> Do wound the bark, the skin of our fruit trees,
> Lest, being over-proud with sap and blood,
> With too much riches it confound itself.

Here, as Professor Dowden admits, " the parallel is remarkably close," but in order to show the " common knowledge of the time," which is to account for it, he cites Holland's *Pliny* to the effect that trees " have a certain moisture in their barkes which we must understand to be their very blood," and he further refers to Pliny (XVII. 24), to the effect that a fir or pine tree must not have its bark " pulled " during certain months, and adds that, " like Shakespeare, Pliny terms the bark the ' skin ' of the tree." Once more, it is remarkable that the reference should be to Pliny, an author with whom, as we know, Bacon was on very familiar terms.*
However, there is a further illustration from Dekker, and a quotation as to " proudly-stirring " sap from Gervase Markham.

* He appears on almost every page of Professor Dowden's article.

Here again, the only question, as it seems to me, is whether this " remarkably close parallelism," considered as one among many, is satisfactorily explained by the fact that other contemporary writers spoke of wounding the bark of trees, and drawing blood. It would, certainly, be more satisfactory, from a Baconian point of view, if we could find in both Bacon and Shakespeare something which could only have been known to those two writers, or to that one writer. But as that is hardly possible we have to consider all the parallel passages together, and ask ourselves whether or not, taken as a whole, they raise the presumption of identity of authorship.

Judge Webb, while denying the allegation that " all that is proper to Shakespeare and to Bacon was the common knowledge or common error of the time," writes as follows : " Whatever inferences may be deduced from the fact, it surely is a fact that the poet, like the philosopher, maintained the theory of pneumaticals, the theory of the transformation of species, the theory that the sun is the efficient cause of storms, the theory that flame is a fixed body, the theory that the stars are fires, and the theory that the heavens revolve around the earth. That the poet should have been as interested as the philosopher in scientific matters is surely a fact worth noting ; and even if they resorted to the store of ' the common knowledge or common error of the time,' it surely is remarkable that they not only resorted to the same storehouse, but selected the same things, and incorporated the same things in their respective writings, and, so far as either their knowledge or their errors in matters of science were concerned, were in reality the same."

And here, since I profess not to be compiling a new " brief for the plaintiff " in the great case of *Bacon v. Shakespeare*, I am content to leave this interesting controversy for further consideration.

G. G.

THE NORTHUMBERLAND
MANUSCRIPT

THE NORTHUMBERLAND
MANUSCRIPT

In the year 1867 there was discovered at old
Northumberland House in the Strand, in a box
which had been for many years unopened, an
Elizabethan manuscript volume containing, amongst
other things, the transcripts of certain compositions
admittedly the work of Francis Bacon. It com-
mences with four speeches written by Bacon in
1592 for Essex's *Device*, viz. : " The praise of
the worthiest virtue " ; " The praise of the worthiest
affection "; "The praise of the worthiest power ";
" The praise of the worthiest person." These
speeches were published in 1870 by Mr. James
Spedding, with an introductory notice of the
manuscript, and a facsimile of its much bescribbled
outside page, or cover, of which more anon. The
speech in praise of knowledge professes to have
been spoken in " A conference of Pleasure," and
Mr. Spedding adopted this as the title of his little
work. The manuscript book is thus described
by him : " It is a folio volume of twenty-two sheets
which have been laid one upon the other, folded
double (as in an ordinary quire of paper) and
fastened by a stitch through the centre. *But*

as the pages are not numbered and the fastening is gone, it may once have contained more, and if we may judge by what is still legible on the much bescribbled outside leaf which once served for a table of contents, there is some reason to suspect that it did." In a note he adds : " One leaf, however—that which would have been the tenth—is missing ; and one, which is the fourth, appears to have been glued or pasted in." It is clear that he included this missing " tenth " leaf in his " twenty-two sheets."

Mr. Spedding, therefore, carefully examined the volume in the condition in which it was when found at Northumberland House, and, as his accuracy is well known, we may be content to rely upon his evidence in this matter. At any rate it is the best that we can now get, for as Mr. Frank Burgoyne, the Librarian of the Lambeth Public Libraries (who in 1904 edited and published a transcript and colotype facsimile of the whole of the contents of the volume) informs us : " Since Mr. Spedding wrote, the manuscript has been taken to pieces and each leaf carefully inlaid in stout paper, and these have been bound up with a large paper copy of his pamphlet entitled ' A conference of Pleasure.' The manuscript in its present condition contains 45 leaves, so Mr. Spedding does not appear to have included the outside page in his enumeration. The pages are not numbered, and there are no traces of stitching, or sewing ; *it is therefore quite impossible even to conjecture what was the number of sheets in the original volume."**

* My italics. The manuscript has been damaged by fire (probably in 1780), the edges of the pages being much scorched and singed.

This statement will be found not unimportant when we come to consider yet another work on these old manuscripts, also published in 1904, by Mr. T. Le Marchant Dowse. Mr. Dowse is anxious to limit the original volume to a quire of 24 sheets. Spedding, he says, " tells us it was a quire of 22 sheets, [Spedding however, only says it was folded double " as in an ordinary quire of paper "] but he omits to take into account the outer sheet, which was of the same fold of paper and served as a cover ; this made 23 sheets. Moreover he tells us leaf 10 was missing (the written matter, however runs on without a break) ; but as leaf 10 must have formed one half of a sheet, the other half, in the latter part of the MS., should also have been missing, consequently the ' quire ' was originally a full and proper quire of 24 sheets."

But as I have already pointed out, Spedding evidently includes the missing leaf, which he numbers " the tenth," in his twenty-two sheets, equally with the leaf which, as he says, " appears to have been glued or pasted in." Mr. Dowse's ingenious attempt to limit the volume to 24 sheets therefore fails, and, in the present condition of the manuscripts, the only safe conclusion is that stated by Mr. Burgoyne, viz., that " it is quite impossible even to conjecture what was the number of sheets in the original volume." But of this more presently.

On the outside page or cover, besides a number of very interesting scribblings, we find a list which has been generally looked upon as a table of contents of the volume as it originally existed. It runs as follows :

BACONIAN ESSAYS

(1) Mr. ffrancis Bacon.
    Of tribute or giving what is dew. [With the four " praises " above mentio/ed.]

(2) Earle of Arundells letter to the Queen.

(3) Speaches for my lord of Essex at the tylt.

(4) A speach for my lord of Sussex tilt.

(5) Leycester's Common Wealth. Incerto autore.

(6) Orations at Graies Inne revells.

(7) . . . Queenes Mate [Probably Letters to the Queen's Majesty]. By Mr. ffrancis Bacon.

(8) Essaies by the same author.

(9) Rychard the Second.

(10) Rychard the Third.

(11) Asmund and Cornelia.

(12) Ile of dogs frmnt [i.e. fragment] by Thomas Nashe.

But, as Mr. Spedding points out, just above the writing, " Earle of Arundells letter to the Queen," stand the words " Philipp against Mounsieur," a title which he says seems to have been inserted afterwards, and is imperfectly legible."* This evidently refers to Sir Philip Sydney's letter to the Queen dissuading her from marrying the Duke of Anjou, which is part of the contents of the volume as it has come down to us. The Gray's Inn Revels are, no doubt, those of 1594-5 of which the history is related in the *Gesta Grayorum*.

Now of this list, besides the four Discourses or " Praises," only four items are found in the volume as it at present exists, viz., the " Speaches for my lord of Essex at the tylt " ; the " Speach for my lord of Sussex at the tilt " ; " Leycester's Common Wealth," and Sir Philip Sydney's letter. The

---

* See Spedding's *Introduction*, p. xix. It is, I believe, contended by some that the word here is not " Philipp," but as Mr. Spedding so read it when the manuscript was very much clearer than it is now, we may, I think, be content to accept his evidence, more especially as close to it, a little to the left, stands the word " Phillipp " still plain for all to read. Mr. Burgoyne, therefore, includes this letter of Sir Philip Sydney among the subjects mentioned in the supposed list of contents.

actual contents of the volume in its present condition
are as follows :*

(1) *Of Tribute, or giving what is due.* By Bacon (1592).
(2) Of Magnanimitie or heroicall vertue. By Bacon.
(3) An Advertisement touching private censure. By Bacon.
(4) An Advertisement touching the controversies of the church of England. By Bacon (written 1589).
(5) A letter to a French gent : touching ye proceedings in Engl. : in Ecclesiasticall causes translated out of French into English by W. W. By Bacon.†
(6) *Speeches for my lord of Essex at the tylt*, viz., five speeches spoken in a *Device* presented by Essex, and performed before Queen Elizabeth in 1595. By Bacon.
(7) *For the Earl of Sussex at the tilt.* By Bacon (1596).
(8) *Sir Philip Sydney's letter to the Queen*, dissuading her from marrying the Duke of Anjou. (1580).
(9) *Leycester's Common Wealth*, imperfect both at beginning and end (printed 1584).

On comparing these two lists we find also that
four of the articles now contained in the volume
are not mentioned in the list on the outer page,
viz. :

No. 2. Of Magnanimitie.
No. 3. Advertisement touching private censure.
No. 4. Advertisement touching the controversies of the Church.
No. 5. Letter to a French gent, etc.

On the other hand if this list was really a list of
the original contents of the volume then eight
articles have disappeared from the book, besides

---

* The items in italics are mentioned in the list on the outside page.
It will be seen that the latest date of any article of the contents is 1596.
Note that six of the nine pieces are by Francis Bacon.

† See Spedding's *Introduction*, p. xvi.

the missing portions of *Leycester's Common-wealth*, viz. :

> (1) The Earle of Arundell's letter to the Queen.
> (2) The Orations at Gray's Inn revels.
> (3) An address or letter to the Queen, by Bacon.
> (4) Essays by Bacon.
> (5) and (6) Shakespeare's plays of Richard II and Richard III.
> (7) Asmund and Cornelia (of which nothing is known).
> (8) The Ile of Dogs, by Thomas Nashe.

Now, on this state of things, Mr. Dowse vehemently contends that the list on the outside cover is not, and never was meant to be a " table of contents." He asserts that all this matter could not have been either accidentally lost, or (as seems much more probable) intentionally abstracted from the volume. First, because he says the volume originally consisted of a quire and no more ; but as I have already said this is a mere conjecture, which in the face of Mr. Spedding's evidence, is quite untenable. Secondly, because, " on the said assumption, the MS, as found, should have shown a considerable bulge, from top to bottom, alongside the fold," and Spedding must have seen this " considerable bulge " if it had been there, and must have mentioned it if he had seen it ! Mr. Dowse goes on to say that there is other " evidence on the point quite sufficient to satisfy reasonable beings," which is an expression commonly used when a writer wishes to imply that those who do not accept his conclusions are not endowed with the reasoning faculty. Mr. Dowse's idea of " evidence " is, as I shall show, somewhat peculiar, but in any case, I do not think many of his readers will be much impressed with the " considerable bulge," or " the silence of Mr. Spedding " line of argument, especially as Mr. Spedding, though not mentioning the " bulge," has definitely put on record his opinion that the volume may have originally included much more matter than it now contains. It is almost certain, for example, that it contained, with the other speeches written by Bacon for Essex's *Device* in 1595, *The Squire's speech in the tilt-yard*, as well as the beginning and the end of *Leycester's Common Wealth*. But let us hear Mr. Spedding. After enumerating the speeches written for this *Device*, which are now contained in the volume (viz., The Hermits fyrst speach : The Hermits second speach : The Soldier's speach : The Squire's speach), he writes : " These are the speeches written by Bacon for a *Device* presented by the Earl of Essex on the Queen's day 1595, concerning which see *Letters and Life of Francis Bacon*, vol. I. pp. 374-386. The principal difference between this copy and that at Lambeth, from which the printed copy was taken, is that this does *not* contain ' The Squire's speech in the tilt-hard," with which the other begins, and *does* contain a short speech from the Hermit—' the Hermitt's fyrst speach '—which seems to be a reply to it. It is possible that the beginning has been lost, *as any number of sheets may have dropped out at this place, without leaving any evidence of the fact.*"

Further on (p. xix), after giving the list of the titles on the outside cover, which he takes to have been a table of contents, Mr. Spedding writes :

" The principal difficulties which I find in it are, first, the absence from the list of all allusion to the *Advertisement touching the controversies of the Church of England*, which can never have been separated from the volume, and has all the appearance of having been transcribed about the same time, and is too large a piece to have been overlooked ; secondly, the absence from the volume itself of all trace of the *Earl of Arundell's letter to the Queen*, which appears in the list, and thirdly, the misplacing of the entry of Sir Philip *Sydney's Letter against Monsieur*, which stands higher in the list than it should. All this however may be explained by a few suppositions, not in themselves improbable, namely that the transcriber of the first five pieces left his list of contents incomplete ; that the transcriber who followed him set down the contents only of his own portion ; that the first sheet or two of his transcript has been lost, and that Sydney's letter had been at first overlooked. I have already observed that the sheet on which the fifth piece ends and what is now the sixth begins, is the middle sheet of the volume ; and therefore if *anything came between these two, it may have been taken out without leaving any traces of itself.* I have noticed also that Sir Philip's letter has no heading, and may therefore have been easily overlooked. Now if we may suppose that the Earl of Arundell's letter, having been transcribed on a central sheet, has dropped out, and that Sir Philip's having been overlooked, the title was entered afterwards in the place where there was most room, we shall find that the first four titles represent correctly the rest of the contents of the volume. . . . The titles which follow have nothing corresponding to them in this manuscript, *but probably indicate the contents of another of the same kind, once attached to this and now lost.*"

Thus Mr. Spedding, who had the great advantage of seeing the manuscripts as they were found in 1867. But Mr. Le Marchant Dowse will have nothing of all this. He speaks loftily of the " folly " of supposing that the list on the outside page was a table of contents. Apparently he cannot tolerate the idea that two plays of Shakespeare, before they found their way into print, should have been transcribed by the same man, and included in the same volume, with certain works of Francis Bacon ! *Id sane intolerandum.* But if not a table of contents what is the meaning of this outside list ? How did it come to be written " at all, at all " ? Well, Mr. Dowse's theory is as follows : The supposed " quire " originally contained only the " Praises." It came into the possession of the Earl of Northumberland. " It then came under the control of somebody (I shall name him hereafter) who jotted down at intervals the titles of other papers which he judged worth copying, or which were of interest as having reference to, or connexion with, or as having been written by, people whom he knew ; but, on the one hand, he probably found it difficult to procure the papers he wanted ; and meanwhile, on the other hand, papers that he had not previously thought of were unexpectedly placed at the Earl's disposal ; and these were copied as they came to hand." According to this theory, therefore, a scribe in the employ of the Earl of Northumberland, entrusted with a paper volume in which four speeches, composed by Bacon for Lord Essex, had been transcribed, and very carefully and beautifully transcribed,* and finding these noted on the outside cover, which up to that point certainly had done duty as a " table of contents," amuses himself by jotting down beneath, and on the same page, the titles of a number of works which he had not in his possession but which he " judged worth copying," or thought of interest, such as the orations at Gray's Inn, and Bacon's *Essays*, and Shakespeare's plays of *Richard II* and *Richard III*. These, on this hypothesis, he was never able to procure, and therefore their titles on the cover stood for nothing, except as reflections of his inner consciousness. But, meanwhile, other papers, " that he had not previously thought of, were unexpectedly placed at the Earl's disposal ; and these were copied as they came to hand." This theory we are asked, nay ordered, to accept on pain of being dismissed as creatures beyond the pale of reason. Quite unappalled by that terrible threat I venture to think that Mr. Dowse's theory is itself unreasonable. I do not think a scribe entrusted with a nobleman's manuscript volume, in which his duty was to enter further transcripts, would be at all likely to act in such a manner. I think it far more reasonable to suppose that these works had been copied or entered, that they were originally included in the volume, the original dimensions of

---

* " The Northumberland House Manuscript," says Spedding, ": is for the most part remarkably clear and correct ; it is very seldom, that there can be any doubt what letter is intended, and the mistakes are very few." See Mr. Burgoyne's Facsimile.

which it is now impossible to estimate, and that they were subsequently abstracted, probably for some very good season. In fact I think the evidence of Mr. Spedding, the eyewitness, is a great deal better than the hypothesis and conjectures of Mr. Dowse.

But the fact is that Mr. Dowse entered upon his investigation with two preconceived ideas. In the first place his purpose was to have a tilt at the Baconians who had founded some arguments on the close juxtaposition of the names, and certain of the works, of Bacon and Shakespeare in this manuscript. And, secondly, his purpose was to find evidence for his preconceived belief that John Davies of Hereford was the " scribbler " who had written so freely on the outside page of the volume. So much Mr. Dowse, unless I much misunderstand him, himself confesses. " The following investigation," he says in his Preface, " was suggested to me by sundry mistaken notions respecting the MSS. hereinafter examined, which had found their way into print, and so had caught my eye from time to time." Mr. Dowse, as will be seen, is violently anti-Baconian, by which I mean that he is not only altogether contemptuous of " the Baconian theory," but also that he entertains a very low conception indeed of the personal character of Francis Bacon. I think, therefore, I have correctly interpreted the meaning of the above extract. Then as to " the writer of the scribble," he says, " in point of fact upon my first scrutiny, several years ago, of Spedding's facsimile, I provisionally formed an opinion as to who the scribbler was." It will be seen, therefore, that Mr. Dowse set out to prove that the scribbler was John Davies, though, of a certainty, the bare inspection of Spedding's facsimile of the outer page of the manuscript could not justify any belief in the matter, and could, at most, only give occasion for the merest guess.

But before we come to the " scribbler " let us examine the scribble, and see what date we can assign to the writings. What Mr. Spedding calls " the title page," forming half of the outside sheet, " which appears to be the only cover the volume ever had," is covered all over with the so-called scribblings. " It contains," says Mr. Dowse, " some two hundred entries, independently of the ' Praises,' and the list of titles." Mr. Spedding, Mr. Dowse, and Mr. Burgoyne have reproduced this leaf in facsimile, and the latter has provided us with a modern script rendering of it. It may be said to be divided into two columns. At the top of the right-hand column stands the name "\ Mr. ffrancis Bacon," followed by the list of " Praises," which again is succeeded by what Mr. Spedding has called the table of contents. At the top of the left-hand column stands the name of Nevill, twice written, and not far below it is the punning motto of the Nevill family, *Ne vile velis.* " Perhaps," says Mr. Burgoyne, " this gives a clue to the original ownership of the volume as it seems to indicate that the collection was written for or was the property of some member of the Nevill family." It is suggested that this was Sir Henry Nevil (1564-1615), Bacon's nephew, and a friend of Essex. Then high up, in the middle of the page, occur the

THE NORTHUMBERLAND MANUSCRIPT

words "Anthony Comfort and consorte," which is, without doubt, as I think, an allusion to Anthony Bacon. Lower down in the left-hand column are the words :

> Multis annis iam transactis
> Nulla fides est in pactis
> Mell in ore Verba lactis
> ffell in Corde ffraus in factis ;

as to which Mr. Burgoyne points out that among the Tenison MSS. at Lambeth Palace is a letter from Rodolphe Bradley to Anthony Bacon in which he writes : " Your gracious speeches . . . be the words of a faithfull friende, and not of a courtiour, who hath *Mel in ore et verba lactis, sed fel in corde et fraus in factis.**

But the most interesting of these writings are those which refer to Shakespeare. In the right-hand column, somewhat below the centre, occurs the reference to a letter to the Queen's Majesty " By Mr. ffrauncis Bacon." Below this we read " Essaies by the same author." Then the name " William Shakespeare," with the word " Shake-spear " just below, at the right-hand edge of the page. Then follows " Rychard the second," with " ffrauncis " close under the word " second." Then " Rychard the third." Then, towards the bottom of the right-hand column, occurs the name " William Shakespeare " thrice repeated,† and besides this we find " Shakespeare," " Shakespear,"

---

* Mr. Dowse says that the only explanation of this entry that he has heard is that it was suggested by Bacon's behaviour in the Essex case. I have, however, heard another, viz., that it is Bacon's own reflection on the deceits and vanities of life.

† " The name of Shakespeare," writes Mr. Spedding (p. xxv.) " is spelt in every case as it was always *printed* in those days, *and not as he himself in any known case ever wrote it.*"

" Shakespe," " Shak " (several times), " Sh "
(several times), " William," " Will," and so on ;
just as we find in other places " Mr. ffrauncis
Bacon," " Mr. Ffrauncis," " ffrauncis," " Bacon,"
etc., several times repeated.

Upon this Mr. Spedding writes : " That Richard
the second, and Richard the third, are meant for
the titles of *Shakespeare's* plays so named, I infer
from the fact—of which the evidence may be seen
in the *facsimile*—that the list of contents being
now complete, the writer (or more probably another
into whose possession the volume passed) has
amused himself with writing down promiscuously
the names and phrases that most ran in his head ;
and that among these the name of *William Shakespeare* was the most prominent, being written eight
or nine times over for no other reason that can be
discerned. That the name of *Mr. Frauncis Bacon*,
which is also repeated several times, should have
been used for the same kind of recreation requires
no explanation ; its position at the top of the page
would naturally suggest it."

But these are not the only Shakespearean
references which we find on this remarkable page.
About the centre occurs the word " *honorificabile-
tudine*," a reminiscence of the " *honorificicabili-
tudinitatibus* " of *Love's Labour's Lost*.   And lower
down in the left-hand column we have,

revealing
day through
every Crany
peepes and . . .
see
Shak

which seems to be an imperfect reminiscence of the line in *Lucrece*, " revealing day through every cranny spies,"* and is a very interesting contemporary notice of the poem which was first published in 1594 with the name " William Shakespeare " subscribed to the dedication addressed to the Earl of Southampton.

Here, then we have the names and the works of Shakespeare and Bacon brought into curiously close juxtaposition in (as it will presently be seen) a contemporary document. Here are speeches and Essays written by Bacon, and Plays by " William Shakespeare," put together in the same volume (*pace* Mr. Dowse), and we find some penman with these two names so much in his mind that he writes them both, either fully or in abbreviated form, many times over on the outside sheet of the paper book.

Now as to the date of these writings, Mr. Spedding states that he could find nothing, either in the " scribblings " or in what remains of the book itself, to indicate a date later than the reign of Queen Elizabeth. Mr. Burgoyne gives reasons for concluding that the manuscript was written not later than January, 1597, and he says " it seems more probable that no part of the manuscript was written after 1596." There are several reasons for assigning this date to the work. One is that the outside list shows that the volume originally contained a copy of Bacon's Essays. These—the ten short essays which appeared in the first edition—

---

* " Peeps " certainly seems better than " spies," and it has been suggested, therefore, that this gives the line as the poet first conceived it, the alteration having been made to meet the exigency of rhyme.

were published in January, 1597,* after having been extensively circulated in manuscript. After they were printed it is not likely that the expensive and imperfect method of copying in manuscript would have been resorted to.† Again the plays of *Richard II* and *Richard III* were first printed in 1597, " and issued," says Mr. Burgoyne, " at a published price of sixpence each." After that date, therefore, it seems reasonable to suppose that they would not have been transcribed, or noted for transcription. It is not unimportant to remember that when they were first issued the name of Shakespeare was not on them. In the editions of 1598, however, the hyphenated name, " William Shake-speare," appears on each, and this is the first appearance of that name on any play. Nash's " Isle of Dogs " referred to in the outside list was produced at Henslowe's theatre in 1597, but never printed. Of course all the contents of the volume may not have been written in one year, and it is impossible to fix the exact date of the scribblings. But if, as it appears only reasonable to believe, the Shakespearean plays were transcribed (or even only noted for trans-cription) before 1597, we have here references to " Shakespeare " as the author of these plays before his name had come before the public as a dramatic author at all, and more than a year before his name appeared on any title page ; and, what is certainly

---

* " Bacon," writes Mr. A. W. Pollard, " as we should expect, reckoning his year from January." The copy in the British Museum was bought *Septimo die Februarii* 39 E. R.

† This argument holds even if, as Mr. Dowse seeks to prove, the transcription was never carried out in the Northumberland volume. No penman would have noted the Essays for future copying if they were already in print.

remarkable, we find this, at that time little known name closely associated with the name of Francis Bacon.

Who was the writer of the scribble ? Mr. Dowse would identify him with John Davies of Hereford, who was born a year after Shakspere of Stratford and died two years after him. This John Davies was of Magdalen College, Oxford, a poet, and, says Mr. Dowse, " a competent scholar." He took up penmanship as a calling, and " became the most famous teacher of his age ; and he taught, not only in many noble and gentle families, but in the royal family itself, for in those days not even nobles and princes were ashamed to write well." How we could wish that William Shakspere of Stratford had been among his pupils ! But what is the evidence that Davies was " the Scribbler "? Let Mr. Dowse state it in his own words : " His numerous sonnets and other poems, as well as his many dedications, addressed to people of note, while friendly, are also respectful and manly (though he could neatly flatter) : and their number shows the extent of the circle in which he moved. Within this circle, or rather a section of it, I felt myself to be, while dealing with the page of scribble ; and that feeling has been amply justified out of the mouth, or rather by the pen of John Davies himself, for his Works show that he was directly and closely acquainted with nearly all the persons his con- temporaries there mentioned ; with some indeed he was friendly and familiar. The overwhelming evidence of this fact *is of itself sufficient to identify Davies as the scribbler* " (p. 8).

This strikes one as rather curious logic. Davies was closely acquainted with nearly all the persons mentioned in " the page of scribble." *Ergo*, Davies wrote the scribble !

I hardly think a judge would direct a jury to pay much attention to " evidence " of this description. I have no prepossessions whatever against John Davies of Hereford. I am perfectly willing to believe that he was " the scribbler " ; but unless some better proof than this can be adduced, I fear we must regard Mr. Dowse's theory as mere hypothesis. However, Mr. Dowse tells us that he has other evidence. He refers to Davies's " Dedicatory and Consolatory Epistle," addressed to the ninth Earl of Northumberland, which is to be found in the Grenville Library at the British Museum. This, he says, is " with some verbal exceptions written in Davies's beautiful court-hand." And he further tells us that " no one who has studied the scribble and then turns to that ' Consolatory Epistle ' can fail to recognise the same hand at a glance." Here I am not competent to express an opinion, for I have not examined the Epistle in question, nor have I seen the original of the Northumberland MS., and even if I had inspected both I fear I should be in no better case, for nothing is more dangerous than this identification by comparison of handwriting. Anyone who has served an apprenticeship at the Bar knows how perilous it is to trust to the evidence of " expert witnesses " in this matter. I well remember a case in which the two most famous handwriting experts of their day, in this country at any rate,

Messrs. Inglis and Netherclift, swore point blank
one against the other, with equal confidence as to
certain disputed handwriting, so that the judge felt
constrained to tell the jury that they must leave the
" expert evidence " out of the question altogether.
In the Dreyfus case too, the experts, the renowned
M. Bertillon included, seem to have come utterly
to grief. One is reminded of the Judge's famous
categories of " liars," viz., " liars, damned liars,
and expert witnesses ! " Therefore I think it well
to cultivate a little healthy scepticism when Mr.
Dowse identifies " at a glance " John Davies's
" beautiful court-hand " with the scribble of the
Northumberland MS. Mr. Dowse quotes Thomas
Fuller to the effect that " John Davies was the
greatest master of the pen that England in his age,
beheld " ; and goes on to say: " His merits are
summarized under the heads of rapidity, beauty,
compactness, and *variety of styles* ; which last he
so mixed that he made them appear a hundred ! "
I think one ought to be more than ordinarily
cautious in judging of the handwriting of a man
who had a hundred different styles. Yet Mr.
Dowse undertakes to tell us which of the entries
on the outer leaf of the volume are by John Davies,
and which by somebody else ! I repeat I am quite
willing to accept John Davies as the scribbler, but
I fear that at present I must regard the hypothesis
as " not proven." I fear Mr. Dowse may have
been a little too anxious to find the verification of
his preconceived opinion, on his " first scrutiny
of Spedding's facsimile," that Davies was the man
who wrote the scribble. However the fact that

Davies seems to have been for some years in the service of Henry Percy, ninth Earl of Northumberland, as teacher of his family (that is, I presume mainly as writing master*), and possibly as copyist lends some probability to Mr. Dowse's surmise.

Mr. Dowse speaks in very bitter terms of Francis Bacon, perhaps unconsciously allowing his bitterness to be accentuated (as we so often find to be the case) by his abhorrence of the Baconian theory of authorship. It is, at any rate, so strong as to lead him into criticism so obviously, and indeed absurdly, unfair as to carry its own refutation with it, and to impair very seriously the value of the critic's judgment. He assumes that Davies wrote the words " Anthony Comfort, and Consorte," though why the writing master, who was, according to the hypothesis, in the service of the Earl of Northumberland at the time, should have made this entry it is rather difficult to conjecture. However, says Mr. Dowse, it " shows that he was aware of the relations subsisting between the two brothers—that Anthony was the companion and support of Francis, the spendthrift, whom to keep out of prison he impoverished himself, and then did not succeed.

* " To Algernoun, Lord Percy," the Earl's son and heir, whom he addresses as " My right noble Pupill and joy of my heart," Davies writes, " The Italian hand I teach you." Would that he could have taught it to William Shakspere of Stratford ! It was in his time, says Mr. Dowse, " fast superseding the old court-hand." It was, certainly, fast superseding the old German, or " Old English," hand in which Shakspere wrote. And the author of *Twelfth Night* must have known the value of that Italian hand which was at that time rapidly " winning its way in cultured society," as Sir Sidney Lee tells us, for does not he make Malvolio say, " I think we do know the sweet Roman hand " ? But Mr. Dowse does not seem to have known the meaning of the term " court-hand," which is a technical term for the scripts employed by lawyers in drawing up charters and other legal documents, and can very seldom be described as " beautiful."

It also suggests a rebuke of the toadyism of Francis in selecting and, *more suo*, grossly flattering the terrible old termagant on the throne as the ' worthiest person ' in preference to such a brother." When we remember that " the praise of his soveraigne " was, with the other speeches, written in 1592, to be spoken at a *Device* presented by Essex before Elizabeth (the idea being, of course, to conciliate the Queen in favour of Essex, and the very fact of Bacon's authorship being concealed), the suggestion that Davies had in his mind to rebuke Bacon for his " toadyism " because of this purely dramatic performance is, I submit, sufficiently absurd. But that is far from being the worst. I make no complaint whatever that Mr. Dowse will have nothing at all to do with Spedding's attempted vindication of Bacon in the matter of Essex, or that he will make no allowance whatever for the exigencies of Bacon's position as counsel in the service of the Crown. Everyone has the right to form his own opinion upon that, as upon other matters of historical controversy. But, says **Mr.** Dowse, in view of the sentiments which Davies entertained with regard to the families of Northumberland and Essex, " we can imagine how he would feel towards those who were instrumental in bringing Essex to the block. . . . The man that did more than anyone else towards securing the death of Essex was Francis Bacon, but the MS. was planned, and probably in great part executed, before that repulsive procedure, or the contents might have been very different." In plain English, Davies, the assumed writer of the scribble, must, after the Essex affair,

have felt nothing but hatred and scorn for Francis
Bacon, and had Essex's death taken place before
this manuscript was planned, and (probably) in
great part executed, " the contents might have been
very different "; the meaning of which is, I suppose,
either that Bacon's works would have been omitted
altogether, or that the writer would have put on
record " a bit of his mind " with regard to the
author. But it so happens that some years after
this, viz., about 1610, Davies published, in his
Scourge of Folly, a sonnet addressed to Bacon
in which he speaks of him in highly eulogistic terms.
How does Mr. Dowse explain this ? I will place
his remarks before the reader, and afterwards quote
the sonnet in full, and then ask judgment on this
very remarkable style of anti-Baconian criticism.
" It seems," writes Mr. Dowse, " that Bacon had
recently made him (Davies) a present of money,
or more probably had paid him lavishly for some
assistance.   But the poet's gratitude takes a singular
form :

> Thy *bounty*, and the beauty of thy Witt
> *Compells* my pen to let fall shining ink !

Further on he speaks of Bacon 'keeping the Muse's
company *for sport* twixt grave affairs '—an apology
for Bacon's amateur verses."
 Now, first of all be it observed that the italics
and the note of admiration in the above quotations
are Mr. Dowse's own contribution.* And what

---

* The word " bounty " indeed, as the other nouns, " Beauty,"
" Bays," etc., is printed in italics in accordance with the practice of the
times. That does not, of course, imply that any extra emphasis is
on the word. Mr. Dowse omits the italics in the case of the word
" beauty," but emphasises " bounty " and " " compells ! "

THE NORTHUMBERLAND MANUSCRIPT

is the suggestion, again to put it into plain English ?
It is that Davies, though in his heart regarding
Bacon with contempt and abhorrence, had accepted
a large sum of money from him, and therefore felt
compelled, however reluctantly, to write a poem in
his honour ! Observe that Mr. Dowse in other
places speaks of Davies in the highest terms, and
cites him as a witness of unimpeachable honesty
and honour in favour of Shakspere, player and
author. Yet he allows his bitter feelings against
Bacon to carry him so far that rather than recognise
what must be plain to every impartial reader, viz.,
that Davies was writing *ex animo* as a friend and
admirer of Bacon, he would have us believe, in
vilification of his own witness, that the poet was
induced by filthy lucre to write entirely insincere,
and, therefore, particularly nauseous flattery of a
man whom he hated and despised !

And now I will set before the reader the sonnet
in extenso (preserving the italics as in the original),
and ask him whether there is any possible reason to
suppose that it is not an honest expression of the
writer's genuine admiration for Bacon :

> To the royall, ingenious, and all learned Knight,
> Sir Francis Bacon.

> Thy *bounty* and the *Beauty* of thy Witt
> Comprisd in Lists of *Law* and learned *Arts*,
> Each making thee for great *Imployment* fitt
> Which now thou hast (though short of thy deserts)
> Compells my pen to let fall shining *Inke*
> And to bedew the *Baies* that *deck* thy *Front*;
> And to thy health in *Helicon* to drinke
> As to her *Bellamour* the *Muse* is wont:

> For, thou dost her embozom ; and dost use
> Her company for sport twixt grave affaires :
> So utterst Law the livelyer through thy *Muse*.
> And for that all thy *Notes* are sweetest *Aires ;*
> *My Muse thus notes thy worth in ev'ry Line,*
> *With yncke which thus she sugers ; so to shine.*

Now this " sugred sonnet " is I think a very remarkable one. Considering the inflated style in use for laudatory poems of the time, it is written in singularly moderate language, and I think no reader, after considering it as a whole, could possibly put upon it the malignant construction suggested by Mr. Dowse, unless his judgment be warped by very bitter prejudice. But it is not only an honest eulogy of Bacon as a man, it is valuable as bearing witness to the fact, doubtless well known to Davies, that Bacon was a poet. Mr. Dowse speaks contemptuously of Davies's " apology for Bacon's amateur verses," but I fear Mr. Dowse's sight is distorted by a fragment of that broken magic mirror whereof Hans Anderson has written so charmingly. Davies drinks to Bacon's health in " Helicon "— not in " the waters of the Spaw," but in " the waters of Parnassus,"

> As to her Bellamour the Muse is wont.

It is true that Bacon was engaged in " grave affaires "—he had been made Solicitor-General in 1607—and therefore, though he wooed the Muse, could only " use her company " by way of recreation in intervals of more serious employment. Nevertheless he is fully recognised as her " Bellamour."

THE NORTHUMBERLAND MANUSCRIPT

We may be grateful to Mr. Dowse for once more calling attention to this very high and remarkable tribute of praise.

Mr. Dowse goes on to cite Davies's testimony—which is here, of course, to be taken very seriously indeed—to the excellence of William Shakspere. " In his ' Microcosmos,' in a stanza beginning ' Players, I love,' Davies singles out Shakespeare and Burbage for his highest admiration. He attributes to them ' *wit* (i.e. intellect), *courage*, *good shape*, *good partes*, and ALL GOOD ! ' "

Now I will again set forth the lines *in extenso* in order that the reader may form his own opinion as to their meaning and evidentiary value. It is to be observed that Davies does not mention Shakespeare (or Shakspere) or Burbage by name, but there are, in a marginal note to the third line, the letters W. S. R. B., which are generally interpreted as bearing reference to those two " deserving men."* Whether he attributes to them all the excellencies so largely writ in Mr. Dowse's interpretation the reader shall judge. Why Mr. Dowse has written the words " all good " in such startlingly large letters I am unable to say, and I really do not think the poet, who according to Mr. Dowse was of a very strict, if not sanctimonious, turn of mind, intended to attribute ALL GOOD to poor Will Shakspere and Dick Burbage ; while as to his being " over exquisite in depreciating their calling," this fault—if fault it be—he certainly shares with all the other writers of his time

---

* I do not know what evidence there is that these initials were written by Davies himself, and were not additions made by some other hand.

concerning the profession and *status* of the Players. Here is the poem published in the *Microcosmos* or " The Discovery of the Little World, with the Government thereof," 1603 :

> *Players*, I love yee, and your *Qualitie*,
> As ye are Men, *that* passtime not abus'd ;
> And some I love for *painting, poesie*,
> And say fell *Fortune* cannot be excus'd,
> That hath for better *uses* you refus'd :
> *Wit, Courage, good shape, good partes*, and all *good*,
> As long as al these *goods* are no *worse* us'd,
> And though the *stage* doth staine pure gentle *bloud*,
> Yet generous yee are in *minde* and *moode*.

Mr. Dowse follows this by a reference to Davies's poem addressed to

> Our English Terence, Mr. Will.
> Shake-speare.*

which appeared, with the sonnet to Bacon already quoted, in the *Scourge of Folly* (1610-11). On this poem Mr. Dowse waxes eloquent. This, he tells us " in short compass gives us a number of important particulars about him [Shakespeare]. Thus, he acted ' kingly parts,' which means lordly manners and bearing and elocution ; and if he had not *played* those parts (the stage again !)† he would have been a fit companion for a King ; indeed he would have *been* a king among the general ruck of mankind. He had then (as now) his detractors, but he was above detraction, and never railed in return ; for he had a ' reigning wit,' i.e. a sovereign intellect."

I will quote this poem also. *The Scourge of Folly* by the way, is, we read, a work " consisting of

---

* Mr. Dowse omits the hyphen.
† This parenthesis is inserted by Mr. Dowse.

Satyricall Epigramms and others." I fancy there is a good deal of the " Satyricall " in the following :

> Some say (good *Will*) which I, in sport, do sing,
> Hadst thou not plaid some Kingly parts in sport,
> Thou hadst bin a companion for a *King ;*
> And, beene a King among the meaner sort.
> Some others raile ; but, raile as they think fit,
> Thou hast no rayling, but a raigning Wit.
> *And* honesty *thou sow'st, which they do reape ;*
> *So,* to *increase their* Stocke *which they do keepe.*

So Davies, singing " in sport," suggests that according to the saying of some, if the Player had not been a Player he might have been a companion for a King (I rather suspect some esoteric meaning here to which, at this date, we cannot penetrate), and have been himself a King " among the meaner sort." As Miss L. Toulmin Smith writes (Ingleby's *Centurie of Prayse*, p. 94) " it seems likely [? certain] that these lines refer to the fact ·that Shakespere was a player, a profession that was then despised and accounted mean." The poem, of course, has some value for the supporters of the Stratfordian faith, for, if Davies is here writing in sober seriousness, and with no ironical *arrière pensée*, it certainly seems to imply that he supposed " Mr. Will Shake-speare, our English Terence," to be identical with player Shakspere. To which the anti-Stratfordian would reply that, if he did so mean, he was misled, as others were, by the use of the pseudonym Shake-speare. Poems and Plays were published in that name " as it was always *printed* in those days, and not as he [Shakspere] himself in any known case ever wrote it."* In any case Davies's lines can hardly be said to be the high eulogy of Player

* Spedding's *Introduction,* p. xxv.

Shakspere that Mr. Dowse would have them to be.*

A word more and I have done with Mr. Dowse. As I have already said, that which I still venture to call the " table of contents," on the outer page of the paper volume, is headed by Bacon's " Of tribute," and a list of his four " Praises." Now, about an inch below the last " Praise " occurs the word *fraunces*, and a little below and to the right of that is the word *turner*. These we are told are " in different hands," though whether or not they are samples of Davies's hundred different styles it would seem rather difficult to say. Mr. Dowse, however, thinks that *fraunces* was written by the copyist of the " Praises," and *turner* by " the scribbler," and that the latter word was " apparently intended to stand as if related in some way to *fraunces*." He then tells us how pondering over this a brilliant idea struck him. In the middle of the reign of James I occurred the murder of Sir Thomas Overbury, instigated by Frances Howard, Lady Essex, and one of this lady's " principal agents " was a Mrs. Anne Turner. What can be clearer than that we have here a reference to these two notorious criminals ? It follows from this that " the MS. was ' knocking about,' or at any rate open for additions to the scribble on the cover, as late as 1615."†

* I have dealt with this Epigram at some length in *Is there a Shakespeare Problem ?* at pp. 295, 353, and Appendix A. p. 559. So far as I know there is no evidence that Davies knew either Dick Burbage or Will Shakespere personally. On March 28, 1603, Bacon wrote to Davies asking him to use his influence with King James in the writer's favour, and concluding with the words, " so desiring you to be good to concealed poets." (Spedding. *Lord Bacon's Letters and Life*, iii. 65.)

† Dowse pp. 4 and 10.

THE NORTHUMBERLAND MANUSCRIPT

This is going to one's conclusion *per saltum* with a vengeance. It is to be observed that *fraunces* is written just under the *ffrauncis* of " Mr. ffrauncis Bacon," and just above that stands " Mr. Ffrauncis." It seems very probable therefore, that *fraunces* is only written as a variety of, or at least suggested by, the name " ffrauncis," though Mr. Burgoyne does not seem to be right in transcribing it in the latter form. The idea that it stands for the " *Christian name* " of Lady Essex, and " *turner* " for the *surname* of her " principal agent " seems an altogether wild one, and I should imagine that no serious critic would seek to fix the date of any part of the scribble by such a hare-brained supposition.*

I turn then from Mr. Dowse's singularly in-judicial tract to Mr. Burgoyne's more sober comment. " As to the penman who actually wrote the manuscript," says Mr. Burgoyne, " nothing certain is known. The writing on the contents page is chiefly in one hand, with occasional words in another, and a few words mostly scrawled across the page at an angle appear to be written by a third. The main body of the work is in two or more hand-writings, and the difference is especially to be noted in ' Leycester's Commonwealth,' which appears to have been written in a hurry, for the writing has been overspaced in some pages and overcrowded in others, as if different penmen had been employed.

* If we were to adopt this theory we should have to put the date for the " knocking about " of the MS. even later than that assigned by Mr. Dowse, for though Overbury's murder was discovered in 1615, Lady Somerset, as she then was, was not committed to the Tower till April, 1616, and it is not probable if *turner* stands for Anne Turner, that that name would be written till after the trial had brought it prominently before the public.

There are also noticeable breaks on folios 64 and 88, and the difference in penmanship on these pages is specially remarkable. This points to the collection having been written at a literary workshop or professional writer's establishment. It is a fact worthy of notice, that Bacon and his brother Anthony were interested in a business of the kind about the time suggested for the date of the writing of this book. Mr. Spedding states :—* " Anthony Bacon appears to have served [Essex] in a capacity very like that of a modern under-secretary of State, receiving all letters which were mostly in cipher in the first instance ; forwarding them (generally through his brother Francis's hands) to the Earl, deciphered and accompanied with their joint suggestions ; and finally, according to the instructions thereupon returned, framing and dispatching the answers. Several writers must have been employed to carry out with promptitude such work as here outlined, and we find in a letter from Francis Bacon to his brother,† dated January 25th, 1594, that the clerks were also employed upon other work.· . . . . 'I have here an idle pen or two . . . I pray send me somewhat else for them to write out besides your Irish collection.' " etc., etc.

In a well-known letter to Tobie Mathew, Bacon writes : " My labours are now most set to have those works, which I had formerly published . . . well translated into Latin by the help of some good pens that forsake me not." In this connection

* *Life of Bacon* vol. i, p. 250-1.
† *Ibid.* vol. i, p. 349.

THE NORTHUMBERLAND MANUSCRIPT

Mr. Burgoyne writes : " It is worthy of notice that in ' The Great Assises holden in Parnassus by Apollo and his Assessours,' printed in 1645, the ' Chancellor ' is declared to be ' Lord Verulam,' and ' Ben Johnson ' is described as the ' Keeper of the Trophonian Denne.' "* " It seems not unlikely," says Mr. Burgoyne, " that this literary workshop, was the source of the ' Verulamian Workmanship ' which is referred to by Isaac Gruter in a letter to Dr. William Rawley (Bacon's secretary and executor) written from Maestricht, and dated March 20, 1655. This letter was written in Latin, and both the original and the translation are printed in ' Baconiana, or certain genuine Remains of Sir Francis Bacon,' London, 1679." Mr. Burgoyne gives the following extract :

" If my Fate would permit me to live according to my Wishes I would flie over into *England*, that I might behold whatsoever remaineth, in your cabinet of the *Verulamian* Workmanship, and at least make my eyes witnesses of it, if the possession of the Merchandize be yet denied to the Publick. . . . At present I will support the Wishes of my impatient desire, with hope of seeing, one Day, those [issues] which being committed to faithful Privacie, wait the time till they may safely see the Light, and not be stifled in their Birth."

This letter, we note in passing, shows us that in the *Verulamian* literary Workshop certain " Merchandize " was produced which was " denied to the public "—that in fact (as we know by other

* We know from Archbishop Tenison's *Remains* that Ben Jonson was one of Bacon's " good pens." *Baconiana* 1679, p. 60.

evidence to have been the case) there were many writings of Bacon " committed to faithful Privacie " —to Rawley e.g.—which were to be kept unpublished till they could " safely see the light," but which, most unfortunately, were lost or destroyed.

The suggestion, therefore, is that this paper volume, now known as the Northumberland MS., was a product of the famous Verulamian Workshop or *Scriptorium*, and Mr. Bompas adopting (with too great facility as I think) Mr. Dowse's hypothesis that " the scribbler " was John Davies of Hereford, and referring to the known fact that the " Praises " were written for Essex's *Device* in 1592, points out that at that date John Davies was only 27 and at the beginning of his career, and that it is " fifteen years later, in 1607, that an entry appears in the Northumberland accounts of a payment showing his employment by the Earl."   Mr. Bompas, therefore, suggests that in 1592 Davies might have been in Bacon's employ ; he seems, however to have overlooked the fact that, according to Mr. Dowse, the " Praises " were *not* written by Davies, since they are " in a totally different hand."* The one fact which emerges is that we really do not know who wrote any part of the Manuscript, but that it was written for Bacon by one or more of his secretaries seems entirely probable, seeing that six of the nine pieces which now form its contents are transcripts of Bacon's works, then unpublished.   How Bacon, or his secretary, came into possession of two

* See articles in the modern *Baconiana* for July, 1904, and April, 1905, on *Bacon's Scrivenery*.

unpublished plays of Shakespeare, is a matter for speculation.

As to the "scribble" itself Mr. Spedding writes: "At the present time, if the waste leaf on which a law stationer's apprentice tries his pens were examined, I should expect to find on it the name of the poet, novelist, dramatic author, or actor of the day, mixed with snatches of the last new song, and scribblings of ' My dear Sir,' ' Yours sincerely,' and ' This Indenture witnesseth.'   And this is exactly the sort of thing which we have here." Mr. Dowse demurs to this, for, says he, " the cases are not parallel : there is nothing trivial or vulgar in our scribbler : he was a serious and even religious man : the subjects that interest him are lofty, and like his acquaintance noble."   I will not offer an opinion on this point, viz., as to whether the scribbler was merely an idle penman, or " a serious and religious " penman, but, however that may be, I do not think that Mr. Spedding's analogy holds good.   " A law stationer's apprentice " might certainly exercise his pen on a " waste leaf " as Mr. Spedding suggests, but an outer sheet of a paper volume in which works of importance, or so considered, were transcribed, the whole volume being stitched together, can hardly be described as a waste leaf.   In days when printing was far less common than it is now such a volume would be valuable.   Moreover, on the outside leaf were written the contents of the volume.   A law stationer's apprentice would hardly dare to exercise his idle pen on the outside skin of a newly-engrossed deed.   I am inclined, therefore, to agree with Mr. Dowse that the scribblings were to a certain extent " serious." There is method in their madness. And they are such " acts of ownership," that the scribbler must have had a complete *dominium* over the document.

I have been long, and I fear, tedious over this curious work, but the more one considers Mr. Dowse's tract the more does one find it provocative of criticism. I will now leave the regions of imagination for those of fact. Whether or not John Davies of Hereford was " the Scribbler " seems to me of comparatively little importance.* What is of importance is this :—We have here an undoubtedly Elizabethan manuscript volume. Its contents, as they have come down to us, are nine articles, out of which seven are by Bacon. It seems, therefore very reasonable to believe that the volume was written for Bacon and was perhaps a product of the " Verulamian workshop." Very possibly it was presented by him either to the Earl of Northumberland, or to Sir Henry Neville, his own nephew. It is quite reasonable to believe that among the contents of the volume, as it originally stood, were the two Shakespearean plays, *Richard II* and *Richard III*. In any case these were noted on the outer leaf either as having been transcribed, or for future transcription. Such note would not, in all probability, have been made after 1597, when these plays were first (anonymously) published, at the price of sixpence each. At that date " Shakespeare " was unknown to the public as

---

* Some think the scribbler was Bacon himself, which, if true, is certainly of no little importance.

THE NORTHUMBERLAND MANUSCRIPT

a dramatic author, for not a play had as yet been published under that name. Here then we have the names and the works of Bacon and Shakespeare associated, in close juxtaposition, in a contemporaneous manuscript. Further, the transcriber of, at any rate, part of the work, writing not idly but with serious thought, exercises his pen by writing the names, or parts of the names of Shakespeare and Bacon, over and over again, on the outside sheet. " William Shakespeare," the author of *Richard II* and *Richard III*, seems to be a name familiar to him, although those plays had not as yet been published, and indeed were not published under the name of " Shake-speare " till 1598. He writes the name of " Shakespeare " " as it was always printed," and not as Shakspere of Stratford " in any known case ever wrote it." And not content with associating thus closely the names of Shakespeare and Bacon, on a volume containing some works by both these writers, if two they really were, he must needs, on the same outer sheet, quote a line, slightly varied, from *Lucrece*, and a word from *Love's Labour's Lost*. No other name of poet, or actor, appears upon " the Scribble " as distinct from the table of contents. It is all either Shakespeare or Bacon.

If a dishonest Baconian could fabricate fictitious evidence in the same way as the forger Ireland did for Shakspere, it seems to me that he might well endeavour to concoct such a document as this. But the Northumberland MS. is an undoubtedly genuine document, and it is but natural that the " Baconians " should make the most of it.—G.G.

FINAL NOTE

THERE is one argument in support of the contention that Bacon was the author of *Venus and Adonis* which seems to me to deserve more attention than it has hitherto received.

It was, I believe, first put forward by the late Reverend Walter Begley, of St. John's College, Cambridge, in his book, *Is it Shakespeare?* *—a work which every one interested in the Shakespeare problem ought to read, because it is replete with both information and amusement, and there is hardly a dull page in it. The argument is derived from the Satires of Marston and Hall, our early English satirists, of the sixteenth century, who wrote in bitter vein the one against the other. Both of them have a good deal to say concerning one *Labeo*, which is a pseudonym for some anonymous writer of the time. Now in 1598 Marsten published a poem founded on the lines and model of *Venus and Adonis*, which he called " Pigmalion's Image " (*sic*)—a love poem, not a satire—and as an appendix to it he wrote some lines " in prayse of his precedent Poem," where " Pigmalion " had, according to the old

* John Murray, 1903.

legend, succeeded in bringing the image he had wrought out of ivory to life, and in this appendix occur the following lines :

> And in the end (the end of love I wot),
> Pigmalion hath a jolly boy begot.
> So Labeo did complaine his love was stone,
> Obdurate, flinty, so relentlesse none ;
> Yet Lynceus knowes that in the end of this
> He wrought as strange a metamorphosis.

Now compare the following lines from *Venus and Adonis* (199-200) :

> Art thou obdurate, flinty, hard as steel—
> Nay, more than flint, for stone at rain relenteth.

Here we have Labeo's complaint almost word for word, and we are reminded that at the end of *Venus and Adonis* there was the " strange metamorphosis " of Adonis into a flower, quite as strange as that of " Pigmalion's Image."

Is it not clear, then, that by Labeo is meant the author of *Venus and Adonis* ? It may be said, of course, that it was not the author, but Venus who complained that Adonis was " obdurate, flinty," and relentless, but that is a futile objection, for Marston evidently puts the words of Venus into Labeo's mouth, and it can only be the author of the poem to whom he alludes.

Who, then, was *Labeo* ? Well, " these University wits," as Mr. Begley writes, " were steeped in Horace, Juvenal, Persius, and Ovid, and thence brought forth a nickname whenever an occasion required it." Now in Horace we read :

> Labeone insanior inter
> sanos dicatur.

FINAL NOTE

and we learn that M. Antistius Labeo was a famous lawyer, who, it is said, by too much free speaking had offended the Emperor Augustus.*

But what more have we about this sixteenth century Labeo ? Well, Bishop Hall in his satires mentions him several times, and reflects upon him as a licentious writer who takes care to preserve his anonymity, and, like the cuttle-fish, involves himself in a cloud of his own making. Thus in the second book of his satires, which he called (after Plautus) *Virgidemiæ*, i.e., a bundle of rods, Hall attacks Labeo in the following words :

> For shame ! write better, Labeo, or write none ;
> Or better write, or, Labeo, write alone.
>
> (Bk. II, Sat. 1)

and he ends this satire thus :

> For shame ! write cleanly, Labeo, or write none.

From these lines we may infer, as Mr. Begley says, that Labeo did not write alone, but in conjunction with, or under cover of, another author, and also that he did not write " cleanly," but in a lascivious style, such as the style of *Venus and Adonis*, it might be.

But there is a further passage in Hall's *Virgidemiæ* (Book IV, Sat. 1) which I must quote :

> *Labeo* is whipp'd and laughs me in the face :
> Why ? for I smite, and hide the galléd place.
> Gird but the Cynick's Helmet on his head,
> Cares he for *Talus* or his flayle of lead ?
>
> Long as the crafty *Cuttle* lieth sure
> In the black *Cloude* of his thick vomiture ;
> Who list complain of wrongéd faith or fame
> When he may shift it to another's name ?

* This Labeo is alluded to as a jurist of eminence in the time of Augustus by Justinian in his *Institutes*. See Sandars's Translation (Longmans, 1869), at p. 18.

It would take too long if, in this note, I were to attempt the explanation of this "Sphinxian" passage, as Dr. Grosart called it, but the general meaning seems clear enough, viz : " I, the Satirist, whip Labeo, but Labeo merely laughs at me, for he knows he can shift the blame, and the punishment, on to another whose name he makes use of, while he himself lies, like the Cuttle, in the Cloud of his own vomiture."*

Then, writes Mr. Begley, " Labeo is the writer of *Venus and Adonis* ; and as there is every reason to think that Marston used the name Labeo because Hall had used it, we are therefore able to infer that Hall and Marston both mean the same man. We, therefore, advance another step, and infer that the author of *Venus and Adonis* did not write alone, that he shifted his work to another's name (certainly a Baconian characteristic), and acted like a cuttle-fish by interposing a dark cloud between himself and his pursuers."

But what proof or evidence is there that Labeo stood for Bacon ? Well, Marston's Satires were published, with his " Pigmalion's Image," in 1598, several months after Hall's first three books of *Virgidemiæ* had appeared, and in his Satire IV, entitled *Reactio*, Marston goes through pretty well the whole list of writers whom Hall had attacked, and defends them, but, curiously enough, he seems to take no notice of Hall's attack on

* Mr. Begley suggests (p. 17) that the Cynic's helmet is an allusion to the Knights of the Helmet, of whom we read in the *Gesta Grayorum*, and, as he writes, we know that Bacon was " responsible for this Device performed at his own Gray's Inn during the year 1594." As to " Talus " and his flail, see Spenser's *Fairy Queen*, Bk. V, Cant. i, st. 12.

Labeo, though that attack was a marked and recurrent one. But, says Mr. Begley, " *Labeo is there*, but concealed in an ingenious way by Marston, and passed over in a line that few would notice or comprehend. But when it *is* noticed it becomes one of the most direct proofs we have on the Bacon-Shakespeare question, and, what is more, a genuine and undoubted contemporary proof." What, then, is that proof? It is found in a line addressed by Marston to Hall :

> What, not *mediocria firma* from thy spite ?
>
> (Sat. IV, 77.)

That is to say : " What, did not even *mediocria firma* escape thy spite ? "—or we might translate : " What, was not even *mediocria* safe (*firma*) from thy spite ? "

" *Mediocria firma*," therefore, stands for a writer, and one who had been attacked by Hall. And who was that writer ? Of this there can, surely, be no doubt. " Mediocria firma " was Bacon's motto, and we find it engraved over the well-known portrait of *Franciscus Baconus Baro de Verulam*, which appears at the commencement of his *Sylva Sylvarum*. Moreover, it is a motto which has never been used except by the Earls of Verulam or the Bacon family. " Mediocria firma," therefore, stands for Bacon. But is " Mediocria firma " identical with " Labeo " ?

Well, " Labeo," as used by Marston, stands for the author of *Venus and Adonis*. Of that, I think, there can be no doubt. And Hall's " Labeo," the elusive author of a lascivious poem, who writes under a pseudonym and who is always prepared to shift the responsibility upon somebody else, seems eminently characteristic of Francis Bacon. And it is Bacon, under the guise of " Mediocria firma," the spiteful attacks upon whom in Hall's Satires are deprecated by Marston. In fine, it seems to be eminently probable, though it cannot be said to be absolutely proved, that " Labeo " and " Mediocria firma " are one and the same.

The above is but a brief outline of the argument put before his readers by the late Walter Begley, and I have no space to elaborate it further in this note. I should like, however, to add one final word. If Bacon was the author of *Venus and Adonis*, then he was also the author of *Lucrece*. Well, for myself, I should not be at all surprised to find that he was, in fact, the author of that long, wearisome, tedious, and pedantic poem, where the outraged matron, " *apres avoir été violée autant qu'on peut l'être*," like Candide's Cunegonde, and " pausing for means to mourn some newer way," at last " calls to mind where hangs a piece of skilful painting, made for Priam's Troy," the contemplation of which leads to a prolonged train of reflection concerning Ajax and Ulysses, Paris and Helen, Hector and Troilus, Priam and Hecuba, etc., etc., all of which is singularly out of place in the mouth of Tarquin's unhappy victim. Nor would I, in this connection, omit to refer to that long and curious and unwanted passage concerning heraldry which we find in an earlier part of the poem (lines 54-72), and upon which Mr. George

FINAL NOTE

Wyndham remarks that : " Whenever Shakespeare in an age of technical conceit indulges in one ostentatiously, it will always be found that his apparent obscurity arises from our not crediting him with a technical knowledge which he undoubtedly possessed, be it of heraldry, of law, or philosophic disputation."

Here, in conclusion, I would advert to a passage in this stilted poem which is curiously illustrative of " Shakespeare's knowledge of a not generally known custom among the ancient Romans." When Tarquin has forced an entry into the chamber of Lucrece, we read : " Night wandering weasels shriek to see him there,"—a line which for a long time puzzled all the commentators. For what could *weasels* be doing in Collatine's house or in Lucrece's chamber ? At last, however, some scholar directed attention to the note on Juvenal's Satire XV, 7, in Mayor's edition, where we learn that some animal of the weasel tribe was kept by the Romans in their houses for some purpose or another ; and referring to Facciolati's Dictionary, we read : " Mustela, γαλῆ, animal quadrupes parvum sed oblongum, flavi coloris, muribus, columbis, gallinis infestum. Duo autem sunt genera : *alterum, domesticum quod in domibus nostris oberrat*, et catulos suos, ut auctor est Cicero, quotidie transfert, mutatque sedem, serpentes persequitur," etc.

The Romans then, it seems, had no knowledge of the domestic cat, and had domesticated an animal of the weasel tribe which they kept in the house to kill mice or it might be snakes, and for other purposes. Now, this is just the sort of out-of-the-way and recondite information which Bacon would have delighted in. But does any sane and reasonable man suppose that Will Shakspere of Stratford had ever heard of the " night-wandering weasel " in an ancient Roman house ? The Baconian authorship of *Venus and Adonis* and *Lucrece*, and, I would add, the *Sonnets*, may be rejected as " not proven," but the idea that these works were written by the player who came to London as a " Stratford rustic " in 1587, is surely one of the most foolish delusions that have ever obsessed and deceived the credulous mind of man. *O miseras hominum mentes, O pectora cœca !*

THE END.